CAMPAIGN 319

IMPHAL 1944

The Japanese invasion of India

HEMANT SINGH KATOCH ILLUSTRATED BY PETER DENNIS
Series editor Marcus Cowper

Osprey Publishing
c/o Bloomsbury Publishing Plc
PO Box 883, Oxford, OX1 9PL, UK
Or
c/o Bloomsbury Publishing Inc.
1385 Broadway, 5th Floor, New York, NY 10018, USA
E-mail: info@ospreypublishing.com

www.ospreypublishing.com

OSPREY is a trademark of Osprey Publishing Ltd, a division of Bloomsbury
Publishing Plc.

First published in Great Britain in 2018

ISBN: PB: 9781472820150
             ePub: 9781472820174
             ePDF: 9781472820167
             XML: 9781472828255

18 19 20 21 22   10 9 8 7 6 5 4 3 2 1

Editorial by Ilios Publishing Ltd (www.iliospublishing.com)
Index by Zoe Ross
Typeset in Myriad Pro and Sabon
Maps by Bounford.com
3D BEVs by The Black Spot
Page layouts by PDQ Digital Media Solutions, Bungay, UK
Printed in China through World Print Ltd

Osprey Publishing supports the Woodland Trust, the UK's leading woodland
conservation charity. Between 2014 and 2018 our donations are being
spent on their Centenary Woods project in the UK.

To find out more about our authors and books visit
www.ospreypublishing.com. Here you will find extracts, author
interviews, details of forthcoming events and the option to sign up for
our newsletter.

DEDICATION

This book is dedicated to Manipur, a place to which I owe so much and one
that I will always consider a home. Manipur and its people were
unexpectedly and for no fault of their own thrust on to the front line of
World War II. It was an experience that had a profound impact on the place
and of which the Imphal battle of 1944 was the apogee. This book is in
tribute to that forgotten experience of Manipur and its inhabitants of
World War II.

ACKNOWLEDGEMENTS

In connection with this book, I wish to thank the following: Robert Lyman
in the UK, for his encouragement and support; Yaiphaba Kangjam in
Imphal, for all his help in ways small and large; and Monalisa Arthur in New
Delhi for her terrific editing skills and for being ever ready to assist. I am
also grateful to: Rana T.S. Chhina at the United Service Institution in New
Delhi for making available several old photos on the Imphal battle;
Narender Yadav of the History Division, Ministry of Defence, India, for
access to some of the war diaries; and Harry Fecitt for sharing Imphal-
related maps from his collection. A special vote of thanks to Marcus Cowper
at Osprey for shepherding me along in finalizing this book. And finally, I
remain ever grateful to my parents, Arjun and Dinky Katoch, for their
advice, backing, and endless patience; and my brother, Charit, and sister-in-
law, Mahisha, for always being supportive.

ARTIST'S NOTE

Readers may care to note that the original paintings from which the colour
plates in this book were prepared are available for private sale.
The Publishers retain all reproduction copyright whatsoever.
All enquiries should be addressed to:

Peter Dennis, Fieldhead, The Park, Mansfield, Notts, UK, NG18 2AT
Email: magie.h@ntlworld.com

The Publishers regret that they can enter into no correspondence upon
this matter.

IMPERIAL WAR MUSEUMS COLLECTIONS

Many of the photos in this book come from the huge collections of IWM
(Imperial War Museums) which cover all aspects of conflict involving Britain
and the Commonwealth since the start of the twentieth century. These rich
resources are available online to search, browse and buy at www.iwm.org.
uk/collections. In addition to Collections Online, you can visit the Visitor
Rooms where you can explore over 8 million photographs, thousands of
hours of moving images, the largest sound archive of its kind in the world,
thousands of diaries and letters written by people in wartime, and a huge
reference library. To make an appointment, call (020) 7416 5320, or e-mail
mail@iwm.org.uk
Imperial War Museums www.iwm.org.uk

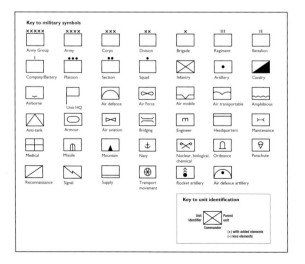

CONTENTS

ORIGINS OF THE CAMPAIGN

At the time of World War II, Imphal was the capital of the princely state of Manipur in the extreme east of India, on its border with Burma (now Myanmar). Ruled by a Maharaja, the state was under British sovereignty. Manipur covered an area of around 22,000 square kilometres (8,500 square miles); to its east and south was Burma, to the west and north was Assam. Imphal lay at the heart of Manipur, in a small, oval-shaped valley some 70km long and 40km wide (45 by 25 miles), surrounded by mountains. The Imphal Valley (also referred to as the Imphal Plain in war accounts), at an altitude of some 800 metres (2,600ft), was the only large stretch of flat ground in the mountainous terrain that defined the India–Burma frontier. As such, it provided a much valued and sought-after ease of passage between the two countries. It is what made Imphal attractive to both the Allies and the Japanese during the Burma Campaign.

Imphal's strategic location came into sharp focus in the first half of 1942. The Japanese rapidly conquered Burma in those months, completing a series of humiliating defeats for the British in the region. Burma was a natural target for the Japanese. First of all, it was rich in natural resources. More importantly, it was from here that the Burma Road originated: the road the Allies were using to send supplies to General Chiang Kai Shek's forces battling the Japanese in China. As the Japanese attack developed from the south, the Burma Road was cut; soon, the sea route out of the country was also closed. The track via the Imphal Valley became the main route out of Burma and into India. It was therefore in the direction of Imphal that the retreating (British) Burma Corps and some 190,000 refugees headed as they escaped the advancing Japanese.

Much like their counterparts in Burma, the British in Manipur and neighbouring Assam were singularly ill-prepared for war, or for receiving the refugees and soldiers that came their way. There was a scramble to get things in order. The track heading south-east out of Imphal to Tamu – just across the Burma border – was broadened and restored in the nick of time. The surviving units of Burma Corps marched into India, ending what is considered the longest retreat in British military history, almost 1,500km (900 miles) in five months. The refugees also passed through Imphal, before continuing into Assam, Bengal and beyond: mainly Indians who had settled in Burma under British rule. Many thousands perished in their desperate march out.

The Japanese twice bombed Imphal from the air in May 1942, emptying the place of its terrified residents. Many had never seen an aeroplane before, let alone suffered an aerial bombing. Fortunately for the British in India, the

Japanese did not continue their advance overland and cross the border. They decided to keep to the east of the Chindwin River in this area. If they had chosen to carry on, there would have been little to stop them. But in cutting the Burma Road, the Japanese had already achieved their main objective. They had also captured vast swathes of territory in the region and now needed to consolidate their hold over it. Imphal, the main entry point into India, was safe for the moment.

In the months that followed, the Japanese did consider an operation to capture Imphal, but this was shelved. The jungle-covered mountains along the India–Burma frontier, with almost non-existent roads, were seen as a daunting obstacle for any large military force to cross. Besides, the Japanese felt they did not have the logistical support and resources to carry through such an offensive. The logic was sound, but the Japanese would never again have such an opportunity: to be able to strike at India when it lay completely undefended in the east. The British and Americans had learnt their lessons about the vulnerability of this region (today called North-East India), and they now set about strengthening its defences. The events of 1942 had also underlined its strategic importance: it was from this region that an overland Japanese attack on India would most likely come and from where an offensive in the opposite direction could be directed; this was also from where supplies would again be sent to the Chinese.

The Allies immediately began work on upgrading the region's infrastructure. Roads were built or improved, the capacity of its railway augmented manifold, and a number of airfields constructed. At the heart of this activity was Manipur. The Imphal Valley's importance as the main entry point into India from Burma had been cemented in 1942. The Allies also began to regard Imphal as the main launch pad for any eventual military offensive into central Burma. It was thus developed as a forward supply base and IV Corps (part of the Eastern Army in India) headquarters moved to Imphal in February 1943. Supply and ordnance depots were constructed and

Japanese tanks are shown crossing a stream via a makeshift bridge during the early campaign in Burma in 1942. The overturned car is described in the original caption as a British Army vehicle. (Getty Images, No. 14876582)

the main roads and tracks out of Imphal were all restored. Most important among them was Manipur's main supply line: the road which went north from Imphal, passed through Kohima (some 137km, or 85 miles, away) in the then-Naga Hills of Assam, and descended to the railway station at Dimapur. But what was to hold the Allies in especially good stead later was the construction of six – including two all-weather – airfields in the Imphal Valley.

While the British and the Americans saw the utility of strengthening India's eastern defences, they had different priorities concerning how to tackle the Japanese in Burma. The Americans' main objective was the restoration of a supply line to the Chinese. They sought to do this first by constructing airfields, clustered in particular around the town of Dibrugarh in Assam, to fly supplies over the Himalayas – nicknamed 'the Hump' – to China's Yunnan province. They also started carving out a road from the town of Ledo in Assam through northern Burma to join up with the last stretch of the old Burma Road. Northern Burma was therefore their main area of interest.

For the British, smarting from their defeat(s) in 1942, taking the fight back to the Japanese in Burma and beyond was of greater interest. The amphibious route to Rangoon – or even better, Singapore – would have been preferred, but the demands on landing craft in other theatres ruled this out in the short term. London was not in favour of retaking Burma by an overland route in what it foresaw would be a long, drawn-out campaign. This view was only strengthened after the failure of a British offensive in the coastal Arakan region of Burma in early 1943. The Americans in any case did not look too kindly at any British effort that might be aimed at recovering the latter's lost colonial possessions in the region. Washington's preference for restoring and continuing the sending of supplies to the Chinese prevailed as the overarching Allied objective for Burma.

But in February 1943 came a British operation that was to have far-reaching consequences for the Allies and the Japanese in Burma. This was the month when Orde Wingate launched Operation *Longcloth*, also known as the first Chindit operation. With its base at Imphal, this involved the sending of some 3,000 men deep behind Japanese lines in Burma. This long-range penetration group set out to disrupt Japanese communication and transport lines heading northwards. Although the military impact of Operation *Longcloth* was limited overall and the force suffered a high casualty rate, the imaginative operation succeeded in boosting Allied morale.

Where it perhaps had the greatest impact was on Japanese thinking and calculations in Burma. It showed, especially to the influential Lieutenant-General Mutaguchi Renya, that large forces could traverse the mountainous India–Burma frontier in pursuit of military

Orde Wingate speaks with his officers in the jungle along the Burmese border with India during the first Chindit operation (Operation *Longcloth*). This operation helped convince Lieutenant-General Mutaguchi of the feasibility of launching an offensive over the mountainous India–Burma frontier to capture Imphal. (Getty Images, No. 50780805)

aims. Mutaguchi had become the commander of Fifteenth Army in March 1943, which came under the newly created Burma Area Army commanded by Lieutenant-General Kawabe Masakazu. Operation *Longcloth* also raised the worrying prospect of an even bigger Allied attack down the same route in the not-too-distant future. To Mutaguchi, such an eventuality had to be pre-empted at the very least, and he began to champion the cause for a Japanese offensive into India.

Mutaguchi's objective of striking at the British in India chimed well with that of Subhash Chandra Bose, who had taken over the reins of the Indian National Army (INA) in Singapore in 1943. The INA had originally been formed with former Indian prisoners of war captured by the Japanese in Malaya and Singapore in 1942. Its objective was to liberate India by defeating the British militarily. While this may have seemed more fanciful at the time of its formation, Bose's takeover had given the INA a greater sense of purpose; thousands of Indian civilians from across South-East Asia had also since flocked to join it. He believed that once the INA had broken through into India, with Japanese help, it would be welcomed by ordinary Indians. It would then be able to advance deep into the country, perhaps even – as its rousing slogan went – march all the way to Delhi. He therefore supported the plan for a Japanese attack on India and offered his army's involvement.

The ever-determined Mutaguchi's lobbying for an offensive eventually paid off. In early January 1944, the Imperial General Headquarters in Tokyo authorized a pre-emptive attack on India. The primary objective of the coming operation – Operation *U Go* – was to be the capture of Imphal. At the same time, by early 1944 the British themselves were looking to push into Burma from Imphal, but this was planned as a limited offensive in support of the Americans' operations in the north. The British offensive was to be led by its Fourteenth Army, which had been created out of the erstwhile Eastern Army in August 1943. It was commanded by Lieutenant-General William J. Slim. The stage was set for a clash between the British Fourteenth Army and the Japanese Fifteenth Army at Imphal in 1944.

The Japanese commander Mutaguchi Renya (second from left) seen here in China in the 1930s. His unit was involved in the Marco Polo Bridge incident of 1937, which precipitated the start of the Second Sino-Japanese War. (Getty Images, No. 561407985)

CHRONOLOGY

8 March — Japanese 33rd Division starts advance.

12 March — Several thousand Japanese spotted few kilometres off Milestone 109 on Tiddim Road.

13 March — Scoones instructs 17th Indian Division to commence withdrawal from Tiddim.

14 March — Japanese 214th and 215th Regiments cut Tiddim Road behind 17th Indian Division at Tuitum Saddle and near Milestones 100 and 109 respectively.

17th Indian Division starts withdrawing from Tiddim.

Yamamoto Force attacks forward positions of 20th Indian Division in Kabaw Valley in strength.

15 March — Japanese 15th and 31st Divisions begin crossing Chindwin River.

37th Indian Brigade, rushed south from Imphal, comes up against first Japanese roadblock near Milestone 100 (Tiddim Road).

16 March — 63rd Indian Brigade recaptures Tuitum Saddle.

Scoones orders 20th Indian Division to start withdrawing from Tamu area.

18 March — Fly-in of 5th Indian Division's two brigades (9th Indian Brigade and 123rd Indian Brigade) from Arakan to Imphal begins.

22 March — 50th Indian Parachute Brigade makes stand at Sangshak.

24 March — Major-General Orde Wingate dies in plane crash after taking off from Imphal.

25 March — 215th Regiment pulls out of positions on Tiddim Road.

26 March — Japanese take Nippon Hill on Shenam Saddle (Tamu–Palel Road) for first time.

50th Indian Parachute Brigade withdraws from Sangshak.

Rearguard of 17th Indian Division blows up bridge over Manipur River on Tiddim Road.

27 March — Fly-in of 5th Indian Division's two brigades from Arakan to Imphal ends.

28 March — 37th Indian Brigade moving south and 48th Indian Brigade advancing north make contact on Tiddim Road.

Honda Raiding Unit arrives at Kangpokpi on Imphal–Kohima Road.

29 March — Imphal–Kohima Road cut by this day.

31 March — Japanese 51st Regiment arrives at Mapao village.

3 April — Japanese 60th Regiment arrives on Imphal–Kohima Road.

4 April — Japanese attack feature near Kameng off Ukhrul Road.

17th Indian Division arrives in Imphal Valley up the Tiddim Road. It moves into Corps reserve in Imphal the next day.

20th Indian Division completes withdrawal from Moreh on Tamu–Palel Road.

6 April — Action at Runaway Hill, for which Abdul Hafiz wins posthumous VC.

7 April	Japanese 51st Regiment attacks Nungshigum.		INA's attack towards Palel Airfield is beaten off.
	Lion Box at Kanglatongbi is evacuated.	7 May	89th Indian Brigade (7th Indian Division), recently flown in from the Arakan, relieves 63rd Indian Brigade at Sekmai.
10 April	17th Indian Division ordered to take over defence of Tiddim Road and Silchar Track with 32nd Indian Brigade (20th Indian Division) under its command.	8 May	Lynch Pimple falls to Yamamoto Force.
13 April	5th Indian Division evicts Japanese from Nungshigum.	10 May	80th Indian Brigade withdraws from Crete West and Japanese take over.
			63rd Indian Brigade attacks Japanese in Potsangbam.
	Japanese attack Sekmai on Imphal–Kohima Road.	11 May	Yamamoto Force occupies part of Scraggy.
	17th Indian Division secures Point 5846 off Silchar Track.	13 May	20th Indian Division and 23rd Indian Division begin switching places on Ukhrul Road and Tamu–Palel Road.
15 April	Japanese blow up bridge on Silchar Track, cutting the last road out of Imphal.	15 May	63rd Indian Brigade secures part of Tiddim Road through Potsangbam.
	23rd Indian Division takes over from 5th Indian Division on Ukhrul Road.		123rd Indian Brigade starts pushing up the Imphal–Kohima Road from Sekmai; 89th Indian Brigade targets hills to the east.
	Japanese attack on Sita in hills north of Tamu–Palel Road fails.		
16 April	Yamamoto Force recaptures Nippon Hill for final time.	16 May	Completion of switchover between 20th Indian Division and 23rd Indian Division.
19 April	Japanese 15th Division abandons efforts to take Sekmai and turns to the defensive.	17 May	48th Indian Brigade establishes Torbung roadblock.
22 April	Yamamoto Force captures Crete East and Cyprus on Shenam Saddle.	19 May	63rd Indian Brigade captures Kha Aimol and Tokpa Khul, and Three Pimple Hill and OP Hill nearby.
	23rd Indian Division's 1st Indian Brigade and 37th Indian Brigade link up near Litan (Ukhrul Road).	20 May	Japanese 214th Regiment attacks Point 2926/Red Hill off Tiddim Road.
28 April	Japanese attack Langgol, east of Palel Airfield.		214th Regiment attacks junction of Silchar Track and Tiddim Road at Bishenpur.
2 May	9th Indian Brigade launches first of multiple attacks on Hump on Mapao–Molvom Range.	21 May	123rd Indian Brigade and 89th Indian Brigade clear Imphal–Kohima Road

	and hills to east between Sekmai and Kanglatongbi.
24 May	Japanese flag flutters on Gibraltar; 37th Indian Brigade recovers feature same day.
	48th Indian Brigade abandons Torbung roadblock.
26 May	214th Regiment attacks Bishenpur again.
29 May	Point 2926/Red Hill recaptured after final attack led by headquarters 50th Indian Parachute Brigade.
1 June	9th Indian Brigade brought to Imphal–Kohima Road from east of Mapao–Molvom Range; switches places with 89th Indian Brigade.
3 June	5th Indian Division ordered to intensify offensive up Imphal–Kohima Road
7 June	Japanese attack Potsangbam and Ningthoukhong.
	Action at Ningthoukhong for which Hanson Victor Turner wins posthumous VC.
	63rd Indian Brigade withdraws from Kha Aimol and Tokpa Khul area.
9 June	Yamamoto Force captures crest of Scraggy.
	Isaac off Imphal–Kohima Road is recaptured from Japanese.
12 June	Last major Japanese attack on North Ningthoukhong.
	Action at Ningthoukhong for which Rifleman Ganju Lama wins VC.
	Imphal–Kohima Road north of Imphal is cleared until Saparmeina.
13 June	5th Indian Division puts in first attack on Liver near Saparmeina.
21 June	Japanese 151st Regiment launches attacks on picquets off Silchar Track.
	Japanese withdraw at night from Liver off Imphal–Kohima Road.
22 June	5th Indian Division and British 2nd Division meet at MS 109 on Imphal–Kohima Road and end siege of Imphal.
26 June	Action at Mortar Bluff for which Subedar Netra Bahadur Thapa wins posthumous VC.
	Action at Mortar Bluff and Water Picquet for which Naik Agan Singh Rai wins VC.
8 July	XXXIII Corps takes Ukhrul.
16 July	Formal, phased withdrawal of Japanese around Imphal begins, as instructed by Mutaguchi.
	17th Indian Division occupies Ningthoukhong Kha Khunou on Tiddim Road.
24 July	Final assault to evict Japanese from Shenam Saddle. Nippon Hill and Scraggy taken.
31 July	XXXIII Corps takes over command of Central front from IV Corps.

OPPOSING COMMANDERS

JAPANESE COMMANDERS

Fifteenth Army at Imphal was commanded by **Lieutenant-General Mutaguchi Renya**. An ambitious man with a strong and dominating personality, Mutaguchi was a division commander during the Japanese defeat of the British in Malaya and Singapore in 1942. The experience had given him a poor view of the latter's military capabilities, an opinion he maintained right through to 1944.

Ironically, Mutaguchi had himself opposed an operation aimed at Imphal when it had first been proposed in 1942, sceptical of the chances of launching a large offensive over the mountains of the India–Burma frontier. He revised his position after the first Chindit operation, then moving to the other extreme: becoming a champion of the cause. Mutaguchi's decision was at least in part motivated by an omnipresent desire for personal grandeur. He hoped to reap the plaudits of a victory at Imphal and any potential repercussions for British rule in India, should the Japanese be able to strike deeper into the country with the INA.

Mutaguchi's ambitions were backed by an imaginative and bold – bordering on reckless – mind. The plan he drew up to strike at India in 1944 had a fair possibility of success. For that to happen, he needed the co-operation of his three division commanders. But Mutaguchi's relations with them were marked by deep mutual dislike and mistrust. The two commanders at Imphal (and one at Kohima) were sceptical of the prospects of Operation *U Go*, and of Mutaguchi's personal motivations for pushing it – and them – so relentlessly.

Lieutenant-General Yanagida commanded the 33rd Division. An intelligent man, he was also considered cautious, perhaps overly so. He felt that Allied capabilities were being underestimated, as was the time it would take to capture Imphal. His relationship with Mutaguchi was particularly poor, to the extent that he was fired halfway through the battle in 1944. His replacement, the ambitious **Major-General Tanaka**, was more in sync with Mutaguchi.

Lieutenant-General Tanaka, one of 17 Japanese generals held as prisoners of war at Insein near Rangoon, passes the time by writing his diary. He had taken over command of the 33rd Division from Lieutenant-General Yanagida more than halfway through the Imphal battle. (IWM, SE 6867)

The 15th Division was commanded by **Lieutenant-General Yamauchi**. Yamauchi was considered polished in his manners and was more of a diplomat than a soldier's general. He had served as the Japanese Military Attaché in Washington DC, and, aware of Allied strength in the region, was concerned about the adequacy of Japanese preparations and logistical support for the operation. He was said to be suffering from tuberculosis. He would also be relieved from command; his replacement, **Lieutenant-General Shibata**, would take over in early July.

Lieutenant-General William J. Slim with Lady Slim at Imphal, where he was knighted by the Viceroy of India, Field Marshal the Viscount Wavell, on 16 December 1944. (IWM, SE 2716)

Another important Japanese officer was **Major-General Yamamoto**. He commanded the 33rd Division's infantry group, which became known as Yamamoto Force. Mirroring the relations between Mutaguchi and his commanders, Yamamoto was in turn equally brusque and impatient in dealing with his subordinates. Thus relations were quite strained within the upper echelons of Fifteenth Army.

ALLIED COMMANDERS

Lieutenant-General Geoffrey Scoones, who commanded IV Corps during the Imphal battle. (IWM, IND 3687)

The situation could not have been more different within Fourteenth Army, and the man who set the tone and led by example was the one who commanded it: **Lieutenant-General William Slim**. A tough, soldier's general, he had a keen sense of the problems his men faced, and he ensured they were well cared for. They, in turn, trusted him implicitly and held him in the greatest regard; to his men, he became known as 'Uncle Bill'.

Slim had taken charge of the newly formed Fourteenth Army in October 1943. Before that, he had been sent to command Burma Corps in the midst of its retreat from Burma in 1942. He had thus been a part of its defeat and withdrawal from the country, an experience he had learnt much from. Slim was a determined man and set about ensuring that the mistakes the British had committed were not repeated in a future fight with the Japanese.

Unlike Mutaguchi, he shared a good rapport with his corps and division commanders, so Slim was able to rely on commanders who shared his vision, and stood ready to implement it. This included **Lieutenant-General Geoffrey Scoones**, who commanded IV Corps at Imphal. Scoones had recently served as Director of Military Operations at General Headquarters in Delhi, and was considered a thinking and analytical officer. This, combined with his cool and calm temperament, was to come in handy in the confused battle at Imphal. He would face some criticism later, however, for not having reacted sooner to the Japanese advance on Imphal from the south.

Among the different division commanders, there was **Major-General Douglas Gracey** of the 20th Indian Division. He knew his division intimately – Gracey had raised, traincd and led this division since its inception in 1942 with the objective of fighting the Japanese. There was **Major-General 'Punch' Cowan**, commander of the 17th Indian Division. This division had fought against the Japanese 33rd Division during the withdrawal from Burma and lost many men in the Sittang Bridge disaster in February 1942. Cowan was a dedicated and inspiring commander who had since done everything he could to ensure his men would be better prepared to fight – and defeat – the Japanese the next time round. There was also **Major-General Ouvry Roberts** of the 23rd Indian Division and **Major-General Harold Briggs** of the 5th Indian Division, whose two brigades were flown into Imphal from the Arakan as reinforcements. All hardy, fighting men, the senior officers had long years of experience, including in World War I. Commanding the respect of their superiors and subordinates alike, they would serve Fourteenth Army well at Imphal.

Major-General D. T. 'Punch' Cowan (centre, wearing spectacles), commander of the 17th Indian Division, at a staff conference. Cowan and the 17th Indian Division were bested by the Japanese 33rd Division in Burma in 1942. Two years later, it was the latter which suffered a heavy defeat at Imphal. (IWM, IND 4689)

INDIAN NATIONAL ARMY COMMANDERS

Compared with the British and the Japanese forces, the INA presence at Imphal was negligible. But the fact that the INA was there at all was thanks to the persuasive man who commanded it: **Subhash Chandra Bose**. The INA had languished for a time before Bose took over in 1943. Well known in India, he had once been the president of the Indian National Congress, the main political party in the country at the time and at the forefront of the struggle for Indian independence. Now on the run from the British in India, Bose had joined hands with the Japanese in his single-minded campaign to free the country from British rule.

Subhash Chandra Bose reviewing soldiers of the Indian National Army (INA) in 1944. (Getty Images, No. 545696233)

Bose rejuvenated the INA and pushed the Japanese for its involvement at Imphal. Even if only a few thousand men would be immediately available, he fought for them to participate as an independent military unit alongside the Japanese. He saw great symbolic and psychological value in their being at the vanguard of the offensive and hoped that a British defeat at Imphal would just be the first, vital step in a much longer march into India for the INA.

OPPOSING FORCES

THE JAPANESE FIFTEENTH ARMY

On the Japanese side at Imphal in 1944 was Fifteenth Army. The army's total strength at the campaign's outset was around 84,000. Of this, at Imphal were two of its infantry divisions, the 15th Division (some 15,000 men) and the 33rd Division (18,000 men). A third division – the 31st (15,000 men) – advanced on Kohima to the north. The remaining 36,000 men were army troops, while another 4,000-odd soldiers arrived as reinforcements as the Imphal battle wore on.

A Japanese infantry division, commanded by a lieutenant-general, had three regiments, which were the equivalent of British brigades. The infantry was often controlled by an Infantry Group, under the command of a major-general. Each of the three regiments was usually commanded by a colonel. Like the British, each infantry regiment in turn had under its command three battalions.

Of the two divisions ordered to capture Imphal, the 15th Division was seriously under-strength and under-gunned when it began its advance. It had been delayed en route to the India–Burma frontier; at one point it had been used to help build a road from northern Thailand to Burma, whilst Allied planes had also bombed a railway line being used to transport it. Now, some units were sent east to help tackle the second Chindit mission (Operation *Thursday*). So the division consisted of only six infantry battalions (instead of nine) in mid-March 1944; it was missing most of its third infantry regiment (the 67th Regiment). Even from this reduced number, one battalion was eventually deployed in support of the 33rd Division. It could muster only 18 guns and its infantry companies were under-manned, with a strength of around 100 men each.

While the Japanese may have lacked numbers, they had certainly built up an impressive reputation by the time they approached Imphal. Their lightning strikes at the British in 1942 had burnished their status as fearsome fighters. They were especially renowned at jungle warfare. They were able to move swiftly through jungle, often unnoticed, using their surroundings to their advantage. It helped that they travelled light, taking with them the bare minimum of supplies and arms.

When on the offensive, the Japanese could be daring. A favourite tactic was to emerge and attack behind their opponents' positions, cutting off their supply lines. The route of escape or withdrawal suddenly blocked, the besieged opposing force would more often than not carry out a disorganized retreat. It was liable to panic, would break out of its encirclement and scatter – only to find the Japanese repeating this manoeuvre farther behind it. This tactic had worked to great effect in 1942. Another strategy was to try to overwhelm the opposing force through *banzai* charges: wave after wave of frontal attacks, with little regard for their own lives.

The Japanese were also dogged defenders par excellence. In jungle and mountainous terrain, they were arguably the best in the world in World War II. Once in place, they would dig in deep, preparing a solid network of bunkers, tunnels and trenches. Many defensive positions were interlocking, making them that much harder to penetrate. The opposing force would be compelled to use everything at its disposal – artillery, infantry, armour and air force – to evict the Japanese from such positions.

Whatever his action, the Japanese soldier displayed an unfailing dedication to the cause. He followed *bushido*, the code of the ancient samurai, and honour and loyalty were paramount for him. He also believed he was fighting to uphold the honour of the Emperor, the cries of *banzai* referring to a wish for his long life. To surrender was not an option; it was preferable to fight unto death.

These characteristics made the Japanese at Imphal in the form of Fifteenth Army a truly formidable force. But because all of this had worked in 1942, it had engendered a certain overconfidence in their own fighting abilities. This was clear from the short timeframe of about a month or so Mutaguchi would set for the capture of Imphal and the lack of adequate attention to ensuring a more secure supply line behind his men.

In terms of artillery, the main infantry support weapons were the 70mm battalion gun, 75mm regimental gun, grenade discharger and 81mm mortar. The Japanese also used mountain, field and medium guns, including 150mm medium howitzers (Model 96), 75mm mountain guns (Model 94) and 105mm field guns (Model 92). In places such as the Tiddim Road, problems of ammunition supply meant that instead of the usual 12 guns, the mountain artillery battalions had only six guns each. The 250mm spigot mortar was also encountered in the Imphal Valley. Anti-tank guns used were the 37mm and 47mm guns. For armoured support, the 14th Tank Regiment had mainly medium (Type 2597) and light (Type 2595) tanks.

In the air, Fifteenth Army had the support of the 5th Air Division of the Japanese Army Air Force. By the time the Imphal offensive began, this included about 131 aircraft, 81 of which were fighters.

THE BRITISH FOURTEENTH ARMY

Fourteenth Army had its IV Corps at Imphal. This consisted of three infantry divisions – the 17th Indian Division (based around Tiddim in Burma), 20th Indian Division (based around Tamu in Burma) and 23rd Indian Division (in reserve in Imphal, with one brigade in the Ukhrul area). Also arrived in March 1944 was the 50th Indian Parachute Brigade.

As the battle unfolded, reinforcements were flown in from the Arakan (where the army's XV Corps was deployed) in the form of two brigades of the 5th Indian Division and one brigade from the 7th Indian Division. The total strength of Fourteenth Army at Imphal during the battle would

Troops of the 5th Indian Division prepare to emplane for Imphal. The fly-in of this division from the Arakan in March 1944 saved the situation for Fourteenth Army at both Imphal and Kohima. (USI-CAFHR)

become about 120,000 – excluding the non-combatants that would be flown out and XXXIII Corps and several of its brigades which would join the fighting in July 1944.

An infantry division was commanded by a major-general, who had under him three brigades, led by brigadiers. Each brigade had three battalions. Several of the brigades at Imphal had a mix of battalions: at times one British battalion together with Indian or Gurkha battalions. The majority of the fighting units at Imphal were Indian and Gurkha.

Among the divisions under IV Corps were those such as the 17th Indian Division that had already fought the Japanese in Burma in 1942. But the British force that would face them at Imphal in 1944 was very different from the earlier avatar: the credit for this went to Lieutenant-General Slim, who had since drawn on that experience to forge his Fourteenth Army into a confident and effective fighting force.

Slim got to work on the morale and material needs of his men. He laid emphasis on rigorous training, especially in the jungle. He understood this is what had made the Japanese soldier adept at jungle warfare. Slim was convinced that with intensive and sustained training, the Fourteenth Army soldier would turn out to be more than a match for the Japanese. Once he became accustomed to marching, surviving and fighting in the jungle, he was less likely to perceive his opponent as some sort of extraordinary fighter. Slim was not disappointed.

Slim also ensured his men were better taken care of. The soldier on the ground had improved access to medical care and a strict programme of malaria prevention was implemented. Attention was devoted to matters of logistics and supplies: he knew these would be crucial in the terrain of the India–Burma frontier. He tried to ensure the supply and communication lines behind his troops were more secure and, as far as possible, shorter.

Crucially, air support and supply was developed and practised, as part of an overall push for better co-ordination between ground and air forces. This sought to counteract the favourite Japanese strategy of encirclement and cutting off supply routes. Surrounded Fourteenth Army units should henceforth be able to hold their ground, fight, and wait for reinforcements to arrive, all the while being dropped supplies from the air.

Fourteenth Army at Imphal was also better armed and had access to a wider range of weaponry than the Japanese. Guns, including 3.7in. howitzers, 6-pdrs and 25-pdrs from several Mountain and Field Artillery Regiment units were at hand, as were anti-tank and anti-aircraft gun units. The 254th Tank Brigade provided armoured support, which included M3 Lee/Grants (medium tanks) and Stuarts (light tanks).

The Royal Air Force's 221 Group, together with the squadrons of Troop Carrier Command, provided support from the air. The Allies had complete superiority over the skies above Imphal and the frontier by the time the

Japanese launched their offensive in 1944. At all times the Allies had, at the very least, three times as many aircraft as those available to the Japanese 5th Air Division for offensive operations; this numerical advantage only increased over time.

THE INDIAN NATIONAL ARMY

The third – albeit much smaller – fighting force at Imphal was the INA. The INA attached great importance to Imphal, even if the initial numbers involved would limit its military value. It was the moment it had been created and waited long for: to try to militarily liberate India from British rule. This was where the 'march to Delhi' would begin and where Indian territory would be captured and start to be administered.

The INA was militarily engaged at Imphal in two ways. The first was through its irregular groups (or units) – a few hundred men attached to each of the Japanese divisions. Their tasks included gathering intelligence; serving as propagandists, with a view to persuading fellow Indians in Fourteenth Army to desert and come over to their side; and accepting those who had surrendered. Others were to be used for sabotage and smaller guerrilla operations, while some would take charge of liberated areas.

The main INA presence was through the 1st Division and its three brigades. But at around 6,000 men, it had far fewer troops than equivalent Japanese or British formations. It also had a certain proportion of civilian recruits that had joined the army since Bose had taken over. Overall, the force was poorly equipped and armed, not adequately trained for the terrain it found itself in and dependent on the Japanese for logistical support and supplies.

ORDERS OF BATTLE[1]

JAPANESE

Fifteenth Army (Lieutenant-General Mutaguchi Renya)

15th Division (Lieutenant-General Yamauchi / Lieutenant-General Shibata)

Advanced Guard
Honda Raiding Unit
    3/67th Battalion (less two companies) (Major Honda)
    Detachment, 15th Engineer Regiment
    Regimental Gun Company, 67th Infantry Regiment
Right Column
    60th Infantry Regiment (less one battalion and two companies)
    (Colonel Matsumura)
    21st Field Artillery Regiment (Less two battalions)
    Two Platoons, 15th Engineer Regiment
    Half of a field hospital
Centre Column
    51st Infantry Regiment (less one battalion and two companies)
    (Colonel Omoto)
    3/21st Field Artillery Battalion
    Detachment, 15th Engineer Regiment
Left Column (assigned to Yamamoto Force from 20 March)
    1/60th Battalion (less one company)
    One battery, 21st Field Artillery Regiment
    Detachment, 15th Engineer Regiment
Units under direct command (Divisional Reserve)
    Headquarters 15th Division
    Two companies, 51st Infantry Regiment
    Three companies, 60th Infantry Regiment
    Two companies, 67th Infantry Regiment
    One composite infantry company
    15th Engineer Regiment (less detachments)
    Medical detachments
    Half of a field hospital
Later Arrivals
    Headquarters 67th Infantry Regiment (May)
    2/67th Battalion (May)
    Remainder of 21st Field Artillery Regiment (June)

33rd Division (Lieutenant-General Yanagida / Lieutenant-General Tanaka)

Right Column (Yamamoto Force)
    Headquarters 33rd Infantry Group (Major-General Yamamoto)
    213th Infantry Regiment (less 1/213th Battalion)
    One company, 1/215th Battalion
    14th Tank Regiment (less one company)
    1st Anti-tank Battalion (less two companies)
    2/33rd Mountain Artillery Battalion
    3rd Heavy Field Artillery Regiment (less one battalion and one
    battery)
    2/18th Heavy Field Artillery Battalion
    One company, 33rd Engineer Regiment
Centre Column
    214th Infantry Regiment (less two companies 3/214th Battalion)
    (Colonel Sakuma)
    1/33rd Mountain Artillery Battalion
    Detachment, 33rd Engineer Regiment
    Headquarters 33rd Division (Following behind)
Left Column
    215th Infantry Regiment (less two companies) (Colonel Sasahara)
    3/33rd Mountain Artillery Battalion
    Detachment, 33rd Engineer Regiment

Reserve (Fort White) Column
    33rd Engineer Regiment (less two companies)
    4th Independent Engineer Regiment
    One company, 215th Infantry Regiment
    One company, 14th Tank Regiment
    18th Heavy Field Artillery Regiment (less one battalion)
    Detachment, 3rd Heavy Artillery Regiment
    3/214th Battalion (less two companies) (from end of May)
Reinforcements
    151st Regiment (less one battalion) (Colonel Hashimoto) (from
    19 June)
    1/67th Battalion (from 17 May)
    2/154th Battalion (from 20 May)
    14th Tank Regiment, 1st Anti-Tank Battalion and 2/18th Heavy
    Field Artillery Battalion were switched to the Tiddim Road from
    Yamamoto Force in May
    For Yamamoto Force
    2/51st Battalion (April)
    Left column, 15th Division

31st Division (Lieutenant-General Kotuku Sato) (for the battle at Sangshak)

Left Column
    Headquarters 31st Infantry Group (Major-General Miyazaki)
    58th Infantry Regiment
    2/31st Mountain Artillery Battalion
    One company, 31st Engineer Regiment
    Signal and medical detachments

Japanese Army Air Force

5th Air Division (General Tazoe)
4th Air Brigade
    50th Air Regiment (Nakajima Ki 43 'Oscar')
    8th Air Regiment (Kawasaki Ki 48 'Lily')
7th Air Brigade
    64th Air Regiment (Nakajima Ki 43 'Oscar')
    204th Air Regiment (Nakajima Ki 43 'Oscar')
    12th Air Regiment (Mitsubishi Ki 21 'Sally')
    81st Air Regiment
62nd Air Regiment (Nakajima Ki 49 'Helen')

Indian National Army (INA)
1st Division (Colonel Mohammad Zaman Kiani)
1st (Subhash) Brigade (less one battalion) (Lieutenant-Colonel Shah
    Nawaz Khan)
2nd (Gandhi) Brigade (Lieutenant-Colonel Inayat Jan Kiani)
3rd (Azad) Brigade (Lieutenant-Colonel Gulzara Singh)
Irregular INA Groups attached to each Japanese division

BRITISH

Fourteenth Army (Lieutenant-General William Slim)

IV Corps (Lieutenant-General Geoffrey Scoones)
Armour
254th Indian Tank Brigade (Brigadier Reginald Scoones)
    3rd Carabiniers (M3 Lee/Grants [Medium tanks])
    7th Cavalry (Stuarts [Light tanks])
    C Squadron, 150th Regiment, Royal Armoured Corps
401st Field Squadron, Indian Engineers
3/4th Bombay Grenadiers, less one company (motorized)

---

1 The main source of these orders of battle is Major-General S. Woodburn Kirby's
    The War Against Japan, Volume III, The Decisive Battles (Uckfield, 1961).

Artillery
8th Medium Regiment, Royal Artillery
67th Heavy Anti-Aircraft Regiment, Royal Artillery
28th Light Anti-Aircraft Regiment, Royal Artillery
78th Light Anti-Aircraft Regiment, Royal Artillery
15th Punjab Anti-Tank Regiment
One battery, 2nd Survey Regiment
Engineers
75th Field Company, Indian Engineers
424th Field Company, Indian Engineers
94th (Faridkot) Field Company, Indian State Forces
305th Field Park Company, Indian Engineers
854th Bridging Company, Indian Engineers
16th Battalion, Indian Engineers
336th Forestry Company, Indian Engineers
3rd West African Field Company
Infantry
9th Jat Machine-Gun Battalion
15/11th Sikh Regiment
Chin Hills Battalion, Burma Army
3rd Assam Rifles
4th Assam Rifles
78th Indian Infantry Company
Kalibahadur Regiment (Nepalese)
One company, Gwalior Infantry, Indian State Forces

17th Indian Light Division (Major-General D.T. 'Punch' Cowan)
Artillery
21st Indian Mountain Regiment
29th Indian Mountain Regiment
129th Light Field Regiment, Royal Artillery
82nd Light Anti-Aircraft/Anti-Tank Regiment, Royal Artillery
Engineers
60th Field Company, Indian Engineers
70th Field Company, Indian Engineers
414th Field Park Company, Indian Engineers
Divisional Infantry
1st West Yorkshire Regiment
7/10th Baluch Regiment
4/12th Frontier Force Regiment
Infantry
48th Indian Brigade (Brigadier Cameron / Brigadier Hedley)
    9th Border Regiment
    2/5th Royal Gurkha Rifles
    1/7th Gurkha Rifles
63rd Indian Brigade (Brigadier Burton)
    1/3rd Gurkha Rifles
    1/4th Gurkha Rifles
    1/10th Gurkha Rifles

20th Indian Division (Major-General Douglas Gracey)
Artillery
9th Field Artillery Regiment, Royal Artillery
114th Jungle Field Regiment, Royal Artillery
23rd Indian Mountain Regiment
55th Light Anti-Aircraft/Anti-Tank Regiment, Royal Artillery
Engineers
92nd Field Company, Indian Engineers
422nd Field Company, Indian Engineers
481st Field Company, Indian Engineers
309th Field Park Company, Indian Engineers
9th Bridging Section, Indian Engineers
Divisional Infantry
4/3rd Madras Regiment
Infantry
32nd Indian Brigade (Brigadier Mackenzie)
    1st Northamptonshire Regiment
    9/14th Punjab Regiment
    3/8th Gurkha Rifles
80th Indian Brigade (Brigadier Greeves)

1st Devonshire Regiment
9/12th Frontier Force Regiment
3/1st Gurkha Rifles
100th Indian Brigade (Brigadier James)
    2nd Border Regiment
    14/13th Frontier Force Rifles
    4/10th Gurkha Rifles

23rd Indian Division (Major-General Ouvry Roberts)
Artillery
158th Jungle Field Regiment, Royal Artillery
3rd Indian Field Regiment
28th Indian Mountain Regiment
2nd Indian Light Anti-Aircraft/Anti-Tank Regiment
Engineers
68th Field Company, Indian Engineers
71st Field Company, Indian Engineers
91st Field Company, Indian Engineers
323rd Field Park Company, Indian Engineers
10th Bridging Section, Indian Engineers
Infantry
1st Indian Brigade (Brigadier King)
    1st Seaforth Highlanders
    1/16th Punjab Regiment
    1st Patiala Regiment, Indian State Forces
37th Indian Brigade (Brigadier Collingridge / Brigadier Marindin)
    3/3rd Gurkha Rifles
    3/5th Royal Gurkha Rifles
    3/10th Gurkha Rifles
49th Indian Brigade (Brigadier Esse)
    4/5th Mahratta Light Infantry
    6/5th Mahratta Light Infantry
    5/6th Rajputana Rifles

50th Indian Parachute Brigade (Brigadier Hope-Thomson / Brigadier Woods)
Engineers
411th (Parachute) Field Squadron, Indian Engineers
Infantry
152nd Indian Parachute Battalion
153rd Gurkha Parachute Battalion
50th Indian Parachute Machine-Gun Company

Flown in from the Arakan in March 1944
5th Indian Division (Major-General Harold Briggs / Major-General Evans)
Artillery
4th Field Regiment, Royal Artillery
28th Jungle Field Regiment, Royal Artillery
56th Light Anti-Aircraft/Anti-Tank Regiment, Royal Artillery
24th Indian Mountain Regiment
Engineers
2nd Field Company, Indian Engineers
20th Field Company, Indian Engineers
74th Field Company, Indian Engineers
44th Field Park Company, Indian Engineers
1st Bridging Section, Indian Engineers
Divisional Infantry
3/2nd Punjab Regiment
Infantry
9th Indian Brigade (Brigadier Salomons)
    2nd West Yorkshire Regiment
    3/9th Jat Regiment
    3/14th Punjab Regiment
123rd Indian Brigade (Brigadier Evans / Brigadier Denholm-Young)
    2nd Suffolk Regiment
    2/1st Punjab Regiment
    1/17th Dogra Regiment

Flown in from the Arakan in May 1944

7th Indian Division
89th Indian Brigade (Brigadier Crowther)
    2nd King's Own Scottish Borderers
    4/8th Gurkha Rifles
    1/11th Sikh Regiment

Arrived from Kohima end of June 1944 (participated in final
    offensive in July)
XXXIII Corps (Lieutenant-General Stopford)
5th British Brigade (Brigadier Alston-Roberts-West) (British 2nd
    Division)
23rd Long Range Penetration Brigade (Brigadier Perowne)
33rd Indian Brigade (Brigadier Loftus-Tottenham) (7th Indian
    Division)
268th Indian Brigade (Brigadier Dyer)

Air Forces

**221 Group Royal Air Force – Imphal (Air Commodore S.F.
Vincent)**
5 Squadron (Hurricane IIC)
11 Squadron (Hurricane IIC)
20 Squadron (Hurricane IID)
28 Squadron (Hurricane IIC)

34 Squadron (Hurricane IIC)
42 Squadron (Hurricane IIC)
60 Squadron (Hurricane IIC)
81 Squadron (Spitfire VIII)
84 Squadron (Vengeance)
110 Squadron (Vengeance)
113 Squadron (Hurricane IIC)
123 Squadron (Hurricane IIC)
136 Squadron (Spitfire VIII)
152 Squadron (Spitfire VIII)
176 Squadron (Beaufighter VIF)
607 Squadron (Spitfire VIII)
615 Squadron (Spitfire VIII)
1 Indian Air Force Squadron (Hurricane IIB/IIC)
7 Indian Air Force Squadron (Vengeance)
9 Indian Air Force Squadron (Hurricane IIC)
Troop Carrier Command – Comilla (Brigadier William Old USAAF)
31 Squadron (Dakota)
62 Squadron (Dakota)
99 Squadron (Wellington X)
117 Squadron (Dakota)
194 Squadron (Dakota)
215 Squadron (Dakota/Wellington)
216 Squadron (Dakota)

Fitters servicing the engine of
a Supermarine Spitfire LF Mark
VIII, 'YB-M', of No. 17 Squadron
RAF, under the protection of a
mobile anti-aircraft gun at the
fair-weather Sapam Airfield.
(IWM, CF 200)

OPPOSING PLANS

Imperial General Headquarters in Tokyo authorized the capture of Imphal in January 1944. Importantly, its directive couched the planned operation as being more defensive in nature, to defend the Japanese in Burma. The underlying rationale was to pre-empt an Allied attack from India, from the most likely direction it would come: Imphal and its vicinity. This is where the first Chindit operation had originated in February 1943, and in the intervening period it had become evident that the British had further strengthened its presence in and around the Imphal Valley. The planned *U Go* offensive into India was thus limited in its scope and aims, aimed more at securing the Japanese in Burma.

Mutaguchi personally had more ambitious plans. While he saw the merit of capturing Imphal and of blocking its main supply route in the hills at Kohima, he did not want to stop there. Instead, he hoped to press his attack farther to include the town of Dimapur, a major supply base through which ran the railway line to Ledo. This was the line the Americans were using to send supplies to the airfields farther north, from where they were being flown to China. Capturing Dimapur would deal a major blow to the Allies, and could potentially open the door to further operations deeper into India. Once they had broken through, the INA was expected to find widespread local support, enabling them to extend the fight to the British in Assam, Bengal and beyond: who knows, perhaps the very foundations of British rule in India could be shaken.

Mutaguchi planned for a swift operation for the capture of Imphal in March 1944. But before then, he planned to attack Fourteenth Army in Arakan in early February. This was aimed at committing British reserves to the Arakan and hopefully diverting their attention from the much larger offensive against Imphal. In the event, this diversionary attack failed, epitomized by the Japanese defeat in the battle of the Admin Box.

Mutaguchi was not deterred. He also sought to outsmart the British in terms of the directions from which his formations would approach Imphal. He knew that IV Corps would expect him to attack Imphal in strength from the south, where the main routes to Tiddim and Tamu in Burma lay. He did plan to attack from this direction and had instructed his 33rd Division to start its advance on 8 March. But he then planned to send the entire 15th Division a week later across the Chindwin River and advance on Imphal from the north. This area was much more sparsely defended, as the British were not expecting a large Japanese force to attack from this direction (the 31st Division was to advance simultaneously on Kohima through here). Mutaguchi – rightly – anticipated that the British would rush reinforcements to the south to stem the 33rd Division's march, leaving the northern approach relatively free to take Imphal.

Imphal was to have fallen by around mid-April. That would be well before the Japanese Emperor's birthday on 29 April. In any case, Imphal had to be taken before the onset of the monsoon in May. The tight deadlines meant that speed was of the essence for the Japanese. It also meant taking on a risky strategy regarding supplies. It was always going to be a challenge to keep tens of thousands of soldiers supplied over the mountains of the India–Burma frontier and across the Chindwin River. Instead of ensuring that this was adequately addressed at the outset, the emphasis on swiftness meant the soldiers were carrying a bare minimum of supplies (some three weeks' worth) and were backed by an unreliable and untested supply line. The expectation was that they would be able to help themselves to Fourteenth Army's supplies from depots and bases that were to fall easily to them. All of these plans depended, of course, on the key assumption that the British, Indian and Gurkha units would be unable to withstand Japanese attacks.

Slim's plans to defend Imphal were predicated on just the opposite. He fully expected Fourteenth Army's men to stand their ground and fight the Japanese onslaught, before beating it back. Indeed, Slim had been seeking just such an opportunity to face off with the Japanese – before entering Burma – and he intended to make it a decisive clash. He wanted this to be on ground of his own choosing, where the Japanese would be strung out with a long and tenuous supply line behind them.

As reports began to filter in of a Japanese build-up on the other side of the Chindwin River, IV Corps's plan was to entice them to a battle in and around the Imphal Valley, in as tight a circle as possible. Two of its divisions were already deployed beyond the India–Burma frontier in the south towards the ends of roads emanating from Imphal: the 20th Indian Division around Tamu on the Tamu–Palel Road and the 17th Indian Light Division (it had only two brigade groups) around Tiddim on the Tiddim Road. The 23rd Indian Division was in reserve in Imphal, with one brigade in the Ukhrul area in the north-east. The Japanese were not expected to pose much of a threat from this latter direction; at most a regiment would approach this way and try to cut the Imphal–Kohima Road.

Once the Japanese offensive began, the two divisions in the south were to withdraw up those roads and go on the defensive around the Imphal Valley. They would thus have short and more secure communication and supply lines behind them, forcing the Japanese to extend themselves over the mountains. Scoones and IV Corps would then have a clear objective to hold the Imphal Valley and destroy the attacking Japanese force.

Timing was key to the British plan. Scoones needed to signal the withdrawal of his two divisions at just the right moment. If it was left too late, the divisions risked getting cut off by the Japanese. Besides then making their own withdrawal a far messier affair, this would draw in the Corps reserve (23rd Indian Division) and leave Imphal, IV Corps headquarters and the main airfields vulnerable. Once the men had successfully withdrawn and assumed their defensive positions, however, it was here around the Imphal Valley that the Japanese attack would first be withstood, then broken up, before Fourteenth Army would go on the offensive.

Ground crews prepare an RAF Hurribomber (Hurricane) at an airstrip around Imphal as a bullock cart trundles across the airfield. (Getty Images, No. 80750090)

THE JAPANESE LAY SIEGE, MARCH TO MID-APRIL 1944

Imphal is a confusing battle to follow. In comparison with the simultaneous battle at Kohima, it also unfolded over a larger area. The British forces and the Japanese fought for almost every square centimetre of a fairly compact space at Kohima – made up of the main ridge and the surrounding heights. Imphal was a vastly more spread-out affair, taking in areas on both sides of the India–Burma frontier. Slim has described the fighting at Imphal as being as bitter as at Kohima, but more diffuse.

In fact, IV Corps was also initially responsible for the Kohima area. When it became clear towards the end of March 1944 that the Imphal–Kohima Road would likely be cut and Scoones would have little operational control over Kohima, it was temporarily placed under the command of the 202nd Line of Communication Area. In early April, the responsibility for Kohima was transferred to XXXIII Corps under Lieutenant-General Stopford in Jorhat (Assam).

In terms of its chronology, the Imphal battle can be broadly understood to have taken place in four stages. The first, from March to mid-April 1944, involved the Japanese laying siege to Imphal and the valley it sits in. The second, from mid-April through to May 1944, had the two sides engaged in a battle of attrition. The tide shifted in favour of Fourteenth Army in the third phase in June 1944, while disaster then befell the Japanese in July as they were routed on all the fronts.

Perhaps the best way to grasp the geography of the Imphal battle is to follow the hub-and-spoke analogy used by Slim. He likened Imphal to the hub of a wheel, with the main roads heading out of the town as its spokes. These routes were used by the Japanese in their advance on Imphal. The bulk of the fighting in 1944 took place simultaneously on or around these routes. Indeed, the town of Imphal itself emerged essentially unscathed from the battle, unlike Kohima, which was devastated.

This book clubs the different routes together under the three broad directions from which the Japanese approached Imphal. There was the south-west, which included the Tiddim Road and the Silchar Track, from where the 33rd Division came; there was the Tamu–Palel Road in the south-east, from where Yamamoto Force (again from the 33rd Division) advanced; and finally there was the vast region to the north and north-east of Imphal, used by the 15th Division. This included – from east to west – the Ukhrul Road, the Iril River Valley, the Mapao–Molvom Range and the Imphal–Kohima Road. We begin with the south-west, where the Japanese first got off the mark.

The Japanese attack on Imphal

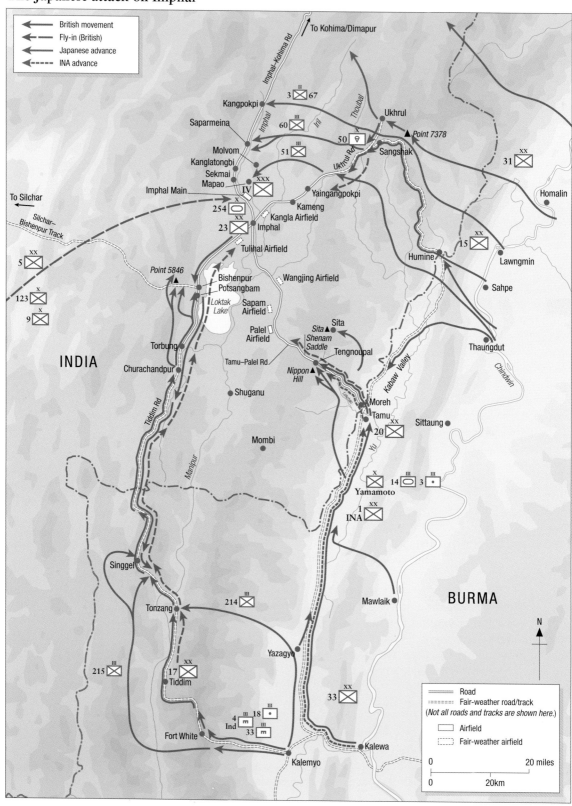

THE SOUTH-WEST

From Tiddim in the Chin Hills of Burma, a road snaked up some 260km (164 miles) to Imphal. For most of this distance, it made its way through steep mountains, crossing the Manipur River and the India–Burma frontier en route. Its last stretch was in the flat Imphal Valley, where it ran in almost straight lines through paddy fields, entering Imphal from the south-west. Beyond Tiddim, the road continued southwards, before turning east towards Kalewa on the Chindwin River.

The 17th Indian Division, under the command of Major-General Cowan, had been deployed around Tiddim in 1943. It had since established itself in the area: building defences, carrying out vigorous patrols and engaging in skirmishes with the Japanese. Its presence in Tiddim was part of the preparatory work for the planned, limited British offensive into Burma. The division was eventually to advance on Kalemyo to give the impression that this was where the main British attack would be from (it was actually to be from Tamu). This would all be in support of American moves in northern Burma, including their advance on the Ledo–Stillwell Road.

By March 1944, it was clear that a Japanese offensive into India was imminent and that it was expected around the 15th of that month. The plan was for the 17th Indian Division to withdraw north up the Tiddim Road to the edge of the Imphal Valley once the attack got under way. It would make its stand there to defend Imphal from this direction. But on this division's front, the columns of the Japanese 33rd Division set off on 8 March – a week before the Japanese 15th and 31st Divisions.

Lieutenant-General Yanagida's division advanced in four columns. Three of these were aimed at Cowan's division. The left column, composed mostly of the 215th Regiment commanded by Colonel Sasahara, was supported by a battalion of mountain artillery and a detachment of engineers. This had crossed the hills to the south of Tiddim, before swinging north. It made for Milestone 100 on the Tiddim Road, near the village of Singgel, and for a large supply depot between Milestones 109 and 110. The centre column, which consisted of the 214th Regiment (less two companies) under Colonel Sakuma, was also supported by a mountain gun battalion and an engineers' detachment. This had moved up the Kabaw Valley; from Yazagyo, it was to turn west and attack Tonzang on the Tiddim Road. This column was to be followed by Yanagida and his headquarters. The objective of these two columns was to cut off the route of withdrawal of the 17th Indian Division and destroy it. They were then to advance on Imphal.

The third column, the reserve (Fort White) column, was formed around the 4th Independent Engineer Regiment and most of the 33rd Engineer Regiment. It was supported by heavy field artillery and a company of tanks. Moving up the road via Tiddim, it was to join the centre column and also subsequently move north to Imphal. The fourth – right – column, an infantry group under the command of Major-General Yamamoto (Yamamoto Force), supported by a tank regiment and most of a heavy field artillery regiment, advanced north up the Kabaw Valley and made for the 20th Indian Division and the Tamu–Palel Road.

Although there had already been reported sightings of groups of Japanese soldiers moving west of the Tiddim Road, and intensified shelling on the forward posts of this division to the east, no order came from Scoones to

A convoy crossing a pontoon bridge on the Tiddim Road in the Chin Hills of Burma in 1944. The Japanese 33rd Division was unable to prevent the withdrawal of the 17th Indian Division up the road to the Imphal Valley in March. (Getty Images, No. 508725348)

Cowan to begin withdrawal. Alarm bells at IV Corps headquarters rang on 12 March only after a confirmed sighting of a large Japanese force a few kilometres off the road at Milestone 109. Not only had the Japanese launched their attack, but they had also already arrived well behind the 17th Indian Division. Scoones spoke to Cowan the next day and gave the order to commence withdrawal. It started the move from Tiddim on 14 March, after laying mines and booby traps. The force consisted of some 16,000 troops, 2,500 vehicles and 3,500 mules. The 63rd Indian Brigade, commanded by Brigadier Burton, was at the front, while the 48th Indian Brigade, under the command of Brigadier Cameron, made up the rear.

But it was too late: the Japanese had cut the Tiddim Road. After putting in attacks against Tonzang, the 214th Regiment (centre column) had captured the Tuitum Saddle to its immediate north by the morning of 14 March. At the same time, the 215th Regiment (left column) had cut the road at several places, including at Milestone 100 and near Milestone 109. The 17th Indian Division would have to fight its way out to Imphal. Over the next fortnight, the main battles to clear the Tiddim Road took place in three places: near Tonzang and the Tuitum Saddle; around the supply depot near Milestone 109; and around Milestone 100.

To help Cowan, Scoones rushed to the Tiddim Road first one brigade – the 37th Indian Brigade – and then a second – the 49th Indian Brigade (from the Ukhrul area) – from the 23rd Indian Division. Given that the third brigade – the 1st Indian Brigade – had been deployed to the north of the Kabaw Valley in support of the fly-in of the brigades of the second Chindit mission (Operation *Thursday*), IV Corps headquarters and Imphal were now left with little protection. The first units of the 37th Indian Brigade came up against the Japanese just short of Milestone 100 by 15 March. Fighting now commenced on both ends: the 37th Indian Brigade southwards on the Tiddim Road and the 17th Indian Division northwards.

For the latter, the men of the Japanese 214th Regiment around Tonzang and on the Tuitum Saddle astride the road were the first hurdles. The saddle overlooked the bridge over the Manipur River, which was vital to the withdrawal of Cowan and his men. Tonzang was being valiantly defended by a composite group of unbrigaded units nicknamed 'Tonforce'. Now it was reinforced by the 63rd Indian Brigade, which had just arrived up the road from Tiddim. The brigade got to work. On 16 March, 'Hurribombers' (Hawker Hurricane fighter-bombers) were called in to bomb and strafe the Tuitum Saddle. Heavy artillery bombardments came next, followed by an infantry attack. The Japanese position, exposed and devoid of overhead cover, was battered, and secured later that day. This allowed the division to cross the bridge over the Manipur River, leaving behind a rearguard. In the

17th Indian Division's withdrawal up the Tiddim Road, March 1944

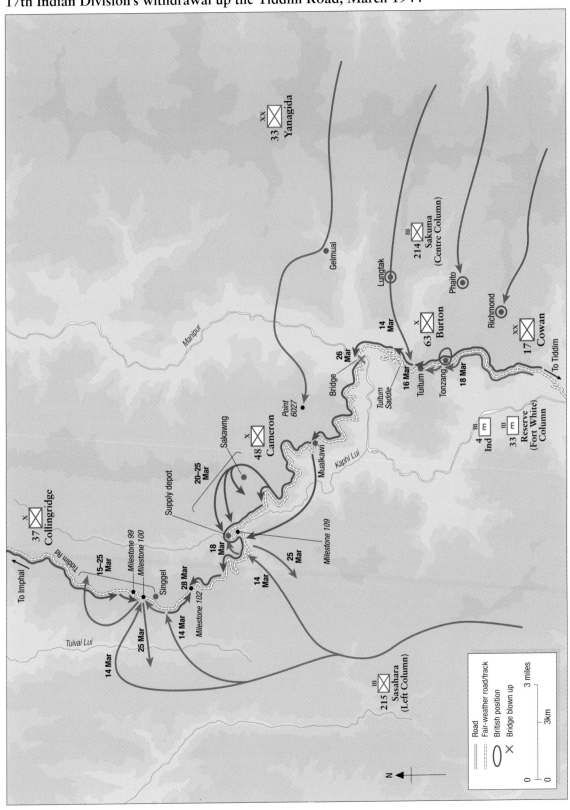

days that followed, the rearguard was subjected to intense assaults on and near the saddle by the 214th Regiment. All of them were beaten off. Notably, four tanks from the reserve (Fort White) column, which had now come up the road, were destroyed after striking a minefield on the road.

Farther north, the division had already bumped up against the next obstacle: the supply depot between Milestones 109 and 110. A battalion of the 215th Regiment had captured the depot on 18 March after only minor resistance. Some 2,700 administrative and support troops manning the depot had been evacuated just before the Japanese closed in. The latter were delighted at capturing the depot: not only had they cut the road behind the 17th Indian Division, but all new supplies were welcome. It would not last.

The 48th Indian Brigade was given the task of evicting the Japanese from the depot and this part of the road. It launched several assaults led by its Gurkha battalions, the 2/5th Royal Gurkha Rifles and 1/7th Gurkha Rifles. The fighting first centred on the village of Sakawng and a ridge just beyond it, which overlooked the supply depot. On 23 March, the 2/5th Royal Gurkha Rifles was well supported by guns and mortars, which plastered the positions, before they moved in with concerted fire from Bren and Tommy Guns in their front rank. The ridge was captured and the Japanese withdrew from the supply depot.

The depot could be secured, however, only after at least two more positions, which overlooked the road from the north, were cleared. This time the 1/7th Gurkhas led the charge. After making their way up steep slopes covered in thick scrub, they put in repeated attacks against strongly defended bunkers. Japanese opposition was fierce, but on the morning of 26 March the Gurkhas found that they had pulled out. The entire depot area around Milestone 109 was secured. Whatever supplies that could be recovered and transported back to Imphal were now taken, while as many as possible that could be of potential value to the Japanese were destroyed. On 26 March, the rearguard withdrew and the bridge over the Manipur River was blown up.

In the meantime, there had also been much action around Milestone 100, where the bulk of the Japanese 215th Regiment had concentrated. The popular Lieutenant-Colonel Irie was in command for the Japanese. Besides preventing Cowan's withdrawal, the Japanese here sought to block off any reinforcements sent from Imphal. For the next ten days it faced off with just such reinforcements in the form of the 37th Indian Brigade (the 49th Indian Brigade was farther back). The fighting was an especially confusing affair: Japanese units came to be sandwiched between British units, who were in turn surrounded by other Japanese units. Slim later described this fighting as 'a Neapolitan ice of layers of our troops alternating with Japanese'. On 23 March, a cannon shell fired by a Hurricane killed Lieutenant-Colonel Irie. Two nights later, the 215th Regiment pulled out.

It later emerged that Lieutenant-General Yanagida had given the order for the 215th Regiment's battalions to pull out of their positions around Milestone 100 and the supply depot area. The story goes that he had received a signal from Colonel Sasahara about the critical situation his regiment was in. Sasahara, in turn, had been reacting to a signal from one of his battalion commanders, Major Sueki. Faced with rapidly depleting ammunition, mounting casualties and attacks on his position near Milestone 109, Sueki had signalled that he would not be able to hold on much longer. He indicated that he would destroy his codes and radio and fight to the end. Sasahara is said to have communicated this and the regiment's resolve to fight to the end to Yanagida.

There is some mystery around this signal, some accounts suggesting the division commander received only the latter half of the message. Either way, Yanagida had had enough. All his reservations about the Imphal offensive came to the fore. He ordered the 215th Regiment to pull out and sent a signal to Mutaguchi about his decision. In this he noted the strength of their opponent, questioned the rationale of the operation and remarked on the impossibility of meeting the deadline. He is supposed to have gone so far as to suggest the suspension of the Imphal offensive. Mutaguchi was livid and berated Yanagida, besides badgering him to proceed swiftly. He resolved to remove him from his command and began passing instructions directly to Yanagida's Chief of Staff. The already-sour relations between the top commanders deteriorated in the face of setbacks.

On 28 March, units of the 37th Indian Brigade heading south made first contact with those of the 17th Indian Division moving in the opposite direction near Milestone 102. The way back to Imphal was now open, barring a roadblock by a major part of the Japanese 2/213th Battalion near the India–Burma frontier. This unit was from Yamamoto Force and had come in from the east. The obstruction was cleared, and by 4 April the 17th Indian Division had arrived in Imphal and gone into Corps reserve.

The 49th Indian Brigade now manned a defensive position astride the road near Torbung. Coming up from Tiddim, this was where the road left the hills and entered the south-western edges of the Imphal Valley. It continued in nearly straight lines from here to Imphal, with the mountains running parallel alongside in the west; to its east for a long stretch was the Loktak Lake. On 9 April, these defences were attacked by the Japanese. Some units also took to the western hills after reaching the valley. The position was shifted north by a few kilometres, but it was becoming clear that it was in danger of being outflanked. On 10 April, the 17th Indian Division again took over the defence of the Tiddim Road and the 32nd Indian Brigade (20th Indian Division) was brought under its command.

After a reconnaissance, Mackenzie, the brigade commander, asked and was authorized to shift the main defensive position farther back to Bishenpur. The village was well located: it was where the hills touched the Tiddim Road to its west; to the east lay the upper reaches of the Loktak Lake. Bishenpur was considered the best place to position a defence of the south-western approach to Imphal. It was also important because from here a track wriggled west over the mountains to Silchar in Assam. Besides the Imphal–Kohima Road, the Bishenpur–Silchar Track (or simply the Silchar Track) was the only other navigable route back out to the rest of India. Unsurprisingly then, it was also of interest to the Japanese. On the night

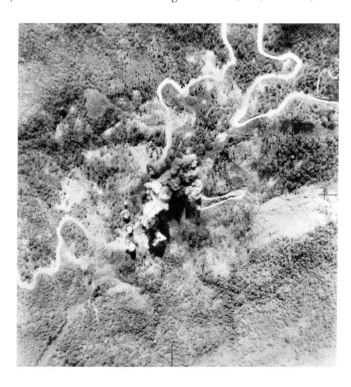

A part of the winding Tiddim Road under attack by aircraft of No. 99 (Liberator) Squadron RAF of the Strategic Air Force, Eastern Air Command, in May 1944. (AWM, P02491.204)

of 14–15 April, a raiding party sent out by Sasahara, together with some INA soldiers, blew up a bridge on the track. They had closed the loop on the south-western approach to Imphal.

The Japanese 33rd Division had failed in their objective of cutting off and destroying the 17th Indian Division, their second encounter after the Sittang Bridge disaster of 1942. This time they had suffered greatly in the process. While the British also had many casualties, one estimate for the Japanese was as high as 2,000 killed or wounded. What was noteworthy was that the surrounded and cut-off Fourteenth Army units had been kept supplied from the air. Ammunition and supplies had been dropped to them on the road, and bombing and strafing runs had assisted the infantry's operations. Such support was almost non-existent for the Japanese. Moreover, there had been no disorganized retreat once the road had been cut behind them: the Fourteenth Army units had stood their ground as required, had fought back and had defeated the Japanese in a straight fight. The template for victory at Imphal in 1944 was set.

THE SOUTH-EAST

The route to Imphal from the south-east was through what was called the Tamu–Palel Road. This was the main road between India and Burma, and by 1944 it was an all-weather one. Tamu in the Kabaw Valley was the last village on the road on the Burma side of the border. Moreh was the first village on the Indian side; from here the road climbed sharply up the mountain range that ran along the frontier, to Tengnoupal village. From Tengnoupal it continued through a saddle, the road winding its way through a collection of hills. This was known as the Shenam Saddle (or Shenam Pass or Shenam Ridge). Then began its twisting descent, via the village of Shenam (locally known as Sinam), to the first village on the road, Palel, on the south-eastern edges of the Imphal Valley.

Present-day view of the Shenam Saddle or Shenam Pass. The British had established defensive positions in these hills, which Yamamoto Force attacked throughout the battle in 1944 as it sought to get through to Imphal from the south-east. Visible here are Gibraltar (right), Malta (left) and the Palel–Tamu Road below. (Author's collection)

From Palel, the road ran through paddy fields all the way to Imphal. By early 1944, there were three airfields along this road. Two of these, Wangjing and Sapam, were fair-weather strips. The Palel Airfield was all-weather. One of only two such airfields around Imphal, Palel was important to the overall defence and sustenance of IV Corps. It was also to be a much sought-after target of the 33rd Division's right assault column – Yamamoto Force.

The defence of this south-eastern approach to Imphal in March 1944 lay with the 20th Indian Division at Tamu. Much like Cowan at Tiddim, Major-General Douglas Gracey's brigades – the 32nd Indian Brigade, 80th Indian Brigade and 100th Indian Brigade – were deployed forward in Burma. They had been aggressively carrying out patrols in the valley and along the banks of the Chindwin River. A large dump had been established at Moreh, the division's administrative area, and stocked with the needs of two divisions. All of this activity had been in preparation for the limited British offensive into Burma that was in the works.

By March 1944, the plan for the 20th Indian Division was to withdraw into three defensive boxes on the Tamu–Palel Road once the Japanese offensive in the opposite direction got under way. The first was to be at Moreh, the second in the Khongkhang–Sibong area, while the third was to be on the Shenam Saddle. A detached battalion protecting the track via Mombi was to withdraw to the Imphal Valley.

Yamamoto Force had set off northwards up the Kabaw Valley for Tamu at the same time as the other columns of the 33rd Division. Major-General Yamamoto commanded an infantry group formed around the 213th Regiment (less one battalion). Two more infantry battalions from the 15th Division were to join him. Importantly, he had in support the 14th Tank Regiment and most of a heavy field artillery regiment. Of the three Japanese forces advancing on Imphal, his had the most firepower and would be backed by the most direct route to the Chindwin River.

Scoones ordered Gracey to withdraw on 16 March. By then there had been confirmed sightings of large-scale crossings of the Chindwin River by the Japanese 15th and 31st Divisions farther north. Since 14 March, Yamamoto Force had also been attacking Gracey's front-line positions to the south. In fact, the only tank-on-tank battle of the campaign took place during this period, pitting a troop of M3 Lee/Grant tanks of the 3rd Carabiniers against some six light tanks of the 14th Tank Regiment. The latter were trounced: four tanks were destroyed and two captured.

While Yamamoto certainly had the armoured and artillery firepower, he was short of infantry at this stage. One battalion (2/213th Battalion, less two companies) had been sent towards Mombi and then west to the Tiddim Road to try to block it near the India–Burma frontier. Another column, formed around the 3/213th Battalion, had been sent in mid-March on a wide outflanking march left to try to block the Tamu–Palel Road (it failed). Only one of the 15th Division's battalions (its left assault column) was on its way, but it would not arrive until later in March. Yamamoto had three companies of infantry left with him and he now proceeded with some caution.

Meanwhile, the 20th Indian Division had been carrying out a controlled withdrawal up the Tamu–Palel Road as per plan. But a problem now arose. Imphal had been stripped of its reserves owing to the 17th Indian Division's

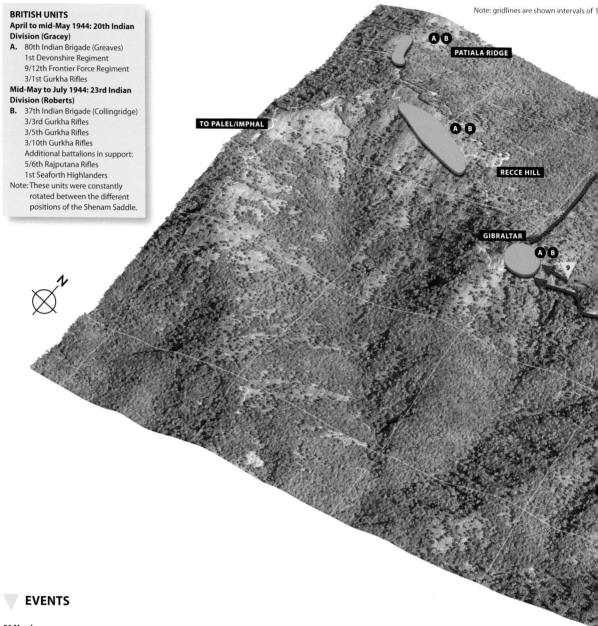

BRITISH UNITS

April to mid-May 1944: 20th Indian Division (Gracey)

A. 80th Indian Brigade (Greaves)
1st Devonshire Regiment
9/12th Frontier Force Regiment
3/1st Gurkha Rifles

Mid-May to July 1944: 23rd Indian Division (Roberts)

B. 37th Indian Brigade (Collingridge)
3/3rd Gurkha Rifles
3/5th Gurkha Rifles
3/10th Gurkha Rifles
Additional battalions in support:
5/6th Rajputana Rifles
1st Seaforth Highlanders

Note: These units were constantly
rotated between the different
positions of the Shenam Saddle.

PATIALA RIDGE

TO PALEL/IMPHAL

RECCE HILL

GIBRALTAR

▼ EVENTS

26 March

1. A small detachment from Yamamoto Force captures Nippon Hill.

4 April

2. The 80th Indian Brigade (20th Indian Division) withdraws up the Tamu–Palel Road. It takes over responsibility for the British defensive positions on the Shenam Saddle.

11 April

3. Following several piecemeal, unsuccessful attempts, Nippon Hill is recaptured by a unit (1st Devons) of the 80th Indian Brigade.

16 April

4. Yamamoto Force again takes Nippon Hill, for the final time. It remains in place until the end of July 1944.

22 April

5. Through fierce infantry attacks, supported by tanks and artillery, the Japanese overrun Crete East by 22 April. Cyprus is left isolated and is soon evacuated; Yamamoto Force moves in. Days of attacks on Crete West follow, but the position is held.

8 May

6. Lynch Pimple is captured by the Japanese. The men on Crete West are cut off from the rest of the 80th Indian Brigade on the Shenam Saddle.

10 May

7. After two weeks of repeated attacks against the feature, Crete West is finally captured by the Japanese after the 80th Indian Brigade withdraws from it.

11 May

8. Wave after wave of Japanese infantry charges are directed at Scraggy through the night of 10 May. Yamamoto Force captures a part of the hill by the morning of 11 May; the Fourteenth Army units hold the crest and the remainder.

24 May

9. After at least one failed attempt in the days just prior, the Japanese again attack Gibraltar on the night of 23 May, including from the north. By the next morning, the crest and parts of the hill have fallen. Within a few hours, however, the Japanese are evicted by units of the 37th Indian Brigade (23rd Indian Division). This is the farthest limit of their advance on the Shenam Saddle and the Tamu–Palel Road.

THE JAPANESE ADVANCE ON THE SHENAM SADDLE (TAMU–PALEL ROAD), 26 MARCH TO 24 MAY 1944

The Shenam Saddle on the Tamu–Palel Road was where the main Japanese advance on Imphal from the south-east was halted. The fighting on this collection of hills at the highest point of the road lasted through the battle and it was the last Japanese stronghold to be cleared in July 1944.

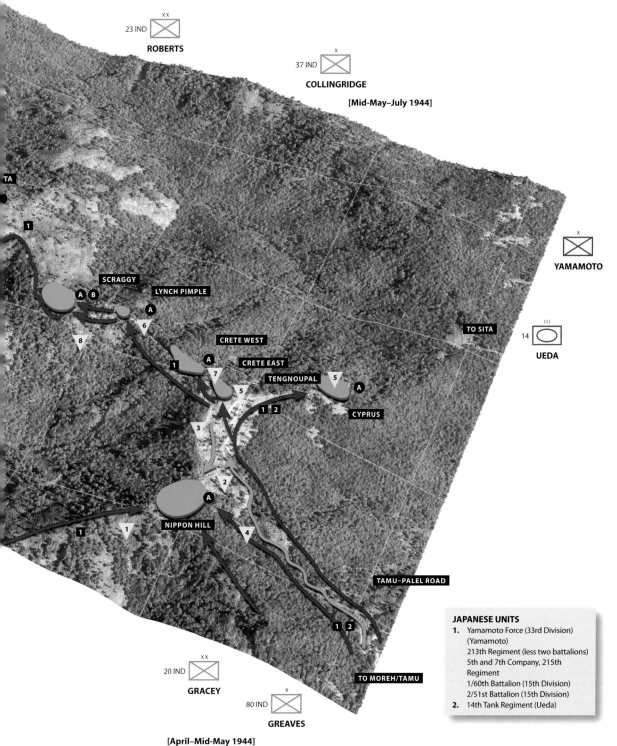

23 IND XX ROBERTS

37 IND X COLLINGRIDGE

[Mid-May–July 1944]

TA

SCRAGGY

LYNCH PIMPLE

YAMAMOTO

TO SITA

14 III UEDA

CRETE WEST

CRETE EAST

TENGNOUPAL

CYPRUS

NIPPON HILL

TAMU–PALEL ROAD

TO MOREH/TAMU

20 IND XX GRACEY

80 IND X GREAVES

[April–Mid-May 1944]

JAPANESE UNITS
1. Yamamoto Force (33rd Division) (Yamamoto)
   213th Regiment (less two battalions)
   5th and 7th Company, 215th Regiment
   1/60th Battalion (15th Division)
   2/51st Battalion (15th Division)
2. 14th Tank Regiment (Ueda)

Men of the Devonshire Regiment sign their autographs on Japanese flags captured at Nippon Hill in April 1944. Yamamoto Force would soon retake the hill and hold it until the end of the battle in July. (IWM, IND 3383)

predicament on the Tiddim Road, and it needed reinforcements. On 25 March, Scoones asked Gracey to send back one of his brigades into reserve. But this would leave his division with only two brigades. Moreh was now to be abandoned and the Shenam Saddle was to become the forward defensive position on the Tamu–Palel Road. The 32nd Indian Brigade withdrew from Moreh on 1 April. It had set the dump on fire; by some estimates at least a million pounds' worth of supplies that had not yet been evacuated were destroyed.

The scene shifted to the hills of the Shenam Saddle. The British had named most of the individual hills, which is where they had their defensive positions, after places in the Mediterranean. The Japanese would come to know some of the same hills by the names of those of their officers who had captured or led assaults on them. There was Crete East or Ikkenya Hill, Crete West or Kawamichi Hill, Scraggy or Ito Hill and Nippon Hill or Maejima Hill. The other key hills were Gibraltar, Recce Hill, Malta, Lynch Pimple and Cyprus.

A unit of Yamamoto Force had managed to capture Nippon Hill on 26 March, but was unable to advance farther. By the time the last of Gracey's troops arrived in early April, a battle for this hill was already in progress. The initial, piecemeal attempts to retake the feature failed. A more robust effort was made on 11 April by the 80th Indian Brigade, which was now responsible for the Shenam Saddle. Three companies of the 1st Battalion, the Devonshire Regiment, were involved. Before they moved in for the attack, Nippon Hill was heavily fired on by the artillery and an air strike was called in. It was thought that very little could have survived the bombardment. And yet, as the Devons closed in on the position, they were greeted with fierce grenade attacks and machine-gun fire. They nevertheless persevered and captured the hill. The Japanese put in three attacks that night, but were repelled.

What was witnessed on Nippon Hill was to be repeated on many occasions around Imphal. Japanese defensive positions would be subjected to intense bombardments, which it was hard to imagine anyone surviving. And yet, time and again, the Japanese would emerge out of the targeted positions and counter-attack. In fact, Nippon Hill was one such place where, even days after it had been recaptured by the British, a lone Japanese soldier would emerge from the rubble and attack. This after being buried for hours, or even days, usually without recourse to food or water.

This behaviour was a measure of the extraordinary capabilities of the Japanese, as defenders in particular, and of their dedication to their cause in general. It was also a testament to the strength of their defences. On features like Nippon Hill, the Japanese had shown themselves to be adept at digging an extensive, deep network of underground tunnels and holes

Present-day view of the two hill ranges east of the Imphal–Kohima Road. In the foreground are the lower hills with features named Isaac, Harry, James and George, and atop which lay Modbung village (or Motbung, as it is locally known) at the time. Visible in the background is part of the Mapao–Molvom Range. (Author's collection)

within their positions. These allowed them to withstand bombardments, while the small openings allowed for a sustained fire to be kept up on anyone who approached.

Yamamoto Force had not yet given up. After another week of attacks, including with the aid of tanks, Nippon Hill fell again on 16 April. It was to stay with the Japanese until the end of July. Meanwhile, they also tried infiltrating through the hills north of the Tamu–Palel Road. In mid-April, one battalion was involved in an attack on a position called Sita. This was repulsed, at the cost of over 300 Japanese casualties.

And so by mid-April 1944, Yamamoto Force was on one end of the Shenam Saddle on the Tamu–Palel Road, with its commander's (Yamamoto) headquarters farther back at Khongkhang. It was firmly ensconced on the main south-eastern route to Imphal.

THE NORTH

The Japanese advance from the south – via the Tiddim Road and the Tamu–Palel Road – did not come as a surprise to Slim and Scoones: these were the main routes from Burma and they had expected Fifteenth Army to use them. It was the strength of the attack from the north of Imphal that was the surprise in March 1944. As all histories of Kohima also note, at most one Japanese regiment was expected to come from this direction and cut the Imphal–Kohima Road. Instead, Mutaguchi sent forth the entire 31st Division, commanded by Lieutenant-General Sato, to Kohima. And moving just south of it was Lieutenant-General Yamauchi's 15th Division: its objective was Imphal.

To understand the fighting to the north of Imphal better, it would help to have an overview of its terrain and main features. Near the northern edge of the Imphal Valley was the town of Imphal itself. To its immediate north-west was IV Corps headquarters. This was in the area called the 'Keep', which also included Imphal Main, the only other all-weather airfield besides Palel. The Imphal–Kohima Road ran parallel to the airfield, before continuing northwards. From Imphal Main to Kangpokpi on this road, some 38km

(24 miles) farther on, the Imphal River (locally called a *turel*) flowed east of the road. The road and the Imphal *turel* ran through a narrow valley for long stretches here, flanked by low-lying hills on both sides.

Surrounding Imphal to the north was an arc of mountains of varying heights. Besides the odd isolated hill, these were the southern tips of north–south running ranges that overlooked the Imphal Valley. Among them was a low-lying range that ran to the immediate east of the Imphal–Kohima Road; of particular interest to the battle in 1944 was the stretch from Sekmai (referred to as Sengmai in military accounts) to Kangpokpi. East of this for a distance was a higher range, with peaks ranging in height from 1,400–1,700m (4,500–5,500ft), on which were perched the villages of Mapao and Molvom (the Mapao–Molvom Range).

The Iril River flowed through a valley to the east of this range and a path ran for several kilometres along the river. Between the river and the Mapao–Molvom Range loomed the Nungshigum massif. Farther east were more mountains; it was through here that a road made its way up to Ukhrul, some 80km (50 miles) from Imphal. Several tracks criss-crossed around Ukhrul. Sangshak village (locally known as Shangshak) lay to its south on a fair-weather road that continued towards Kamjong and Humine, on the border with Burma.

There were few passes through the high and jungle-covered mountains on the India–Burma frontier in this area – and certainly nothing like the Shenam Saddle and the all-weather Tamu–Palel Road. This is why it was not anticipated that the Japanese would – or even could – send in forces in any significant numbers through here. Ironically enough, as with the Tiddim Road, some of the roads and tracks they did end up using in their offensive (such as the Sangshak–Kamjong–Humine one) had only recently been improved by the British.

The 15th Division (and 31st Division) started advancing across the Chindwin on 15 March, a week after the 33rd Division made its move – as per Mutaguchi's plan. He had correctly guessed that Scoones would have rushed his reserves southwards from Imphal by this time to deal with the threat from Yanagida. It was the right moment to attack a vulnerable Imphal from the north. At the outset, Scoones had deployed just one brigade – the 49th Indian Brigade – of the 23rd Indian Division in the Ukhrul area. As it was rushed off to the Tiddim Road on 16 March, its place was taken by the recently arrived 50th Indian Parachute Brigade. Under the command of Brigadier Hope-Thomson, it

Present-day view of what was the main defensive position of the 50th Indian Parachute Brigade at Sangshak village (or Shangshak, as it is known locally) in March 1944. (Author's collection)

was now made responsible for a vast unguarded area through which an entire division was heading towards Imphal, and part of a division towards Kohima.

Indeed, soon heading for Ukhrul was the left assault column of the 31st Division. This was formed around its 31st Infantry Group, commanded by Major-General Miyazaki, and included the 58th Regiment. En route it had clashed with the forward units of the 50th Indian Parachute Brigade deployed on some of the peaks on the approach to Ukhrul, such as Point 7378. It now became aware of the brigade's presence at Sangshak, which is where its forward units had fallen back to and where Hope-Thomson soon concentrated his force. Miyazaki deemed them as being too close to his force's rear and attacked Sangshak. But the 31st Division should never have gone to Sangshak, for the village lay south of Ukhrul and out of its area of responsibility (which was Ukhrul and beyond). Yamauchi's 15th Division was supposed to be responsible for Sangshak and below.

The battle at Sangshak raged from 22 to 26 March. The defenders of the 50th Indian Parachute Brigade grimly held a position of some 550m by 275m (600 yards by 300 yards) that was not even ringed by barbed wire. The Japanese fired the guns of their mountain artillery battalion on the small position and launched waves of infantry attacks. It was clear that the defenders would not be able to hold on forever. The order from Imphal to withdraw was received on the evening of 26 March, and later that night the defenders slipped away.

Sangshak had delayed the advance of the 31st Division's left column to Kohima, but it had also held up some units of the 15th Division bound for Imphal as it lay directly in the line of advance of Yamauchi's 60th Regiment (his right column). When the latter arrived at the village, they found Sato's men already embroiled in the fight. After waiting for the battle to conclude and, finally, a terse exchange with Miyazaki, Yamauchi's men launched their own attack on Sangshak on the last day. This was quickly beaten off and no further attempt was made.

Low aerial view of the Imphal area looking north. Visible here is the all-weather Imphal Main Airfield and the Imphal–Kohima Road to its immediate west. (IWM, MH 4168)

By the time the defenders of Sangshak withdrew, the 60th Regiment's timetable for advancing on Imphal had been thrown off by a few days. Any delay would have affected the tight schedule Mutaguchi had set for capturing Imphal. But that imposed by the battle at Sangshak would prove especially costly. It prevented one of Yamauchi's assault columns (and himself) from arriving on time north of Imphal, and gave Scoones and Slim an extra few days to get Imphal's defences in order.

Fortunately for Fourteenth Army at Imphal and Kohima, Slim had set in motion a move by then that would make all the difference to their defence. He had foreseen that reinforcements would be needed at both places and had already requested them. But Cowan's difficulties on the Tiddim Road and the rushing of Imphal's reserves to its assistance had injected a particular urgency to Slim's request. Getting reinforcements over from the Arakan by road would take too long. They would have to be flown in; and immediately. He requested some 25–30 Dakotas from Vice-Admiral Mountbatten. The only available aircraft were those being used in the Americans' Hump route between Assam and China. The SEAC Commander knew that diverting those aircraft required authorization from the US Chiefs of Staff in Washington, a process that would take some time. But he went ahead and unilaterally ordered their diversion.

Mountbatten's intervention came just in the nick of time. From 18 to 27 March, the 5th Indian Division's 9th and 123rd Indian Brigades were flown to airfields in the Imphal Valley; its 161st Indian Brigade would subsequently

An M3 Lee/Grant tank crosses a river north of Imphal to meet the Japanese advance in March 1944. The Lee/Grants and Stuarts of the 254th Indian Tank Brigade provided invaluable support to the infantry across the Imphal battlefields in 1944. (Getty Images, No. 154419419)

be flown to Dimapur. Around Imphal, men deplaned and were rushed immediately to counter the Japanese threat from the north and north-east. It was the first time in history that an entire division had been flown from one battlefield to another. The first few days after their arrival were a little chaotic, with units arriving at different airfields and having to regroup. In the weeks ahead, these men would face the 15th Division as it sought to break through into Imphal.

Men of the West Yorkshires and the 10th Gurkha Rifles, together with tanks, advance along the Imphal–Kohima Road. The fight to open the road northwards from Imphal was a long, hard-fought one and required close co-ordination between the infantry and armour. (IWM, IND 3469)

Yamauchi's division was making its way in four columns and an advanced guard. The latter's infantry component was a battalion (less two companies) from the 67th Regiment (3/67th) under Major Honda. The right column was formed around the 60th Regiment (less one battalion and two companies) and was commanded by Colonel Matsumura, while the centre column was made up of the 51st Regiment (less one battalion and two companies) under Colonel Omoto. The units under the direct command of the division (divisional reserve), including Yamauchi's headquarters, followed behind the right column. The 1/60th Battalion was in the left column, but this was dispatched south in support of Yamamoto Force.

The advanced guard, also known as the Honda Raiding Unit, was tasked with cutting the Imphal–Kohima Road near 'Mission' (Kangpokpi). It passed via the Ukhrul area – and so avoided the battle at Sangshak – and reached the road on 28 March. It went on to blow a bridge near Kangpokpi. By the next day, the road had been cut.[2]

The right column's (60th Regiment) initial orders were to attack Imphal from the north-west. Held up by the battle at Sangshak, it finally arrived on the Imphal–Kohima Road on 3 April (instead of the end of March). Its units started moving down the road and in the hills alongside. It made for the supply depot about 1.5km (one mile) north of Kanglatongbi. The 221 Advance Ordnance Depot was the largest in the Imphal area. As Japanese pressure on the road increased, its men and some of the most valuable supplies, including ammunition and explosives, were moved into a defensive area at Kanglatongbi known as Lion Box.

In similar moves around the Imphal Valley, self-contained, self-sufficient defensive 'boxes' had been formed, with the basic minimum of provisions to hold out if required for about ten days. These were to defend against possible Japanese attack and protect important facilities, in particular the six airfields around Imphal. The boxes were garrisoned mostly by administrative and support personnel, as well as by RAF ground troops in the case of the main airfields.

---

2   There are two, differing accounts of when the bridge was blown. One claims that it was late into the night of 28 March, while another dates it to the night of 29 March. Either way, the road had been cut by 29 March.

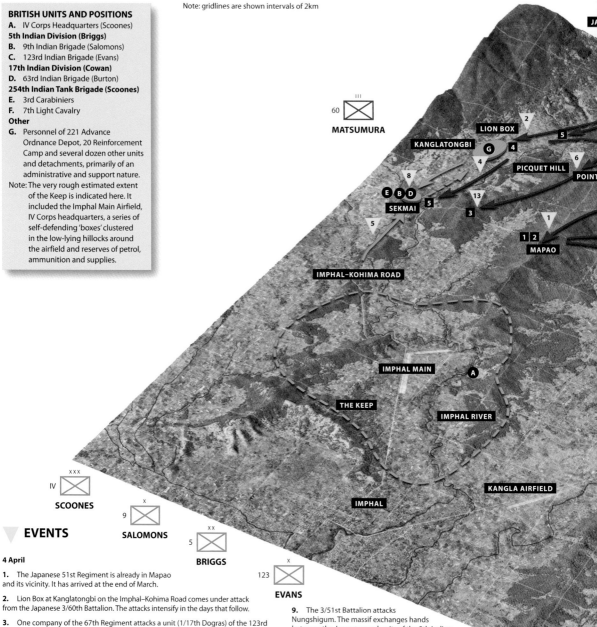

Note: gridlines are shown intervals of 2km

BRITISH UNITS AND POSITIONS
A. IV Corps Headquarters (Scoones)
5th Indian Division (Briggs)
B. 9th Indian Brigade (Salomons)
C. 123rd Indian Brigade (Evans)
17th Indian Division (Cowan)
D. 63rd Indian Brigade (Burton)
254th Indian Tank Brigade (Scoones)
E. 3rd Carabiniers
F. 7th Light Cavalry
Other
G. Personnel of 221 Advance Ordnance Depot, 20 Reinforcement Camp and several dozen other units and detachments, primarily of an administrative and support nature.
Note: The very rough estimated extent of the Keep is indicated here. It included the Imphal Main Airfield, IV Corps headquarters, a series of self-defending 'boxes' clustered in the low-lying hillocks around the airfield and reserves of petrol, ammunition and supplies.

60 | MATSUMURA

LION BOX
KANGLATONGBI
PICQUET HILL
POINT
SEKMAI
MAPAO
IMPHAL–KOHIMA ROAD
IMPHAL MAIN
THE KEEP
IMPHAL RIVER
KANGLA AIRFIELD
IMPHAL

IV | SCOONES
9 | SALOMONS
5 | BRIGGS
123 | EVANS

▼ EVENTS

4 April

1. The Japanese 51st Regiment is already in Mapao and its vicinity. It has arrived at the end of March.

2. Lion Box at Kanglatongbi on the Imphal–Kohima Road comes under attack from the Japanese 3/60th Battalion. The attacks intensify in the days that follow.

3. One company of the 67th Regiment attacks a unit (1/17th Dogras) of the 123rd Indian Brigade on a hill off the Ukhrul Road, south of the village of Kameng. A fierce counter-attack on the Japanese follows, involving the infantry, as well as tank and artillery fire. Almost the entire company is wiped out.

5 April

4. Units of the 9th Indian Brigade, supported by tanks of the 3rd Carabiniers, start patrolling forward from Sekmai to Lion Box to assist in its defence.

5. After withdrawing from the Tiddim Road, the 63rd Indian Brigade reinforces Sekmai.

6 April

6. Moving through the hills east of the Imphal–Kohima Road, the 2/60th Battalion has taken Point 3813 and its immediate vicinity by now.

7. The 51st Regiment is already on the move eastwards towards Nungshigum, as ordered by the 15th Division commander. Some elements of 3/51st Battalion capture a hill near Nungshigum. For fighting to his death to recover it (Runaway Hill), Jemadar Abdul Hafiz of the 3/9th Jats, 9th Indian Brigade, wins the Victoria Cross.

7 April

8. As its defence becomes untenable in the face of mounting Japanese assaults, the evacuation of Lion Box is ordered.

9. The 3/51st Battalion attacks Nungshigum. The massif exchanges hands between the Japanese and units of the 9th Indian Brigade (3/9th Jats) in the days that follow, before the Japanese retake it and firmly dig in by 11 April.

8 April

10. Also ordered eastwards by Yamauchi, elements of the 3/60th Battalion take up positions around the villages of Tingsat, Molvom and the surrounding heights. Meanwhile, the Honda Raiding Unit comes down the Imphal–Kohima Road to the Kanglatongbi area.

9 April

11. The 1/51st Battalion attacks Point 4057 and its vicinity north of the Ukhrul Road. However, it withdraws to the hills farther north by mid-April after being counter-attacked.

13 April

12. An all-out counteroffensive is directed at Nungshigum – using the air force, artillery, infantry from the 123rd Indian Brigade (1/17th Dogras) and armour (3rd Carabiniers). The Japanese are evicted later that day.

13. Units of the 60th Regiment and the Honda Raiding Unit target Sekmai and its surrounding area, but they are repulsed. Another attack some five days later is also beaten back.

THE JAPANESE ATTACK FROM THE NORTH, 4–13 APRIL 1944

In the first two weeks of April 1944, the Japanese advanced towards Imphal through and around the arc of hills skirting the north of the town.

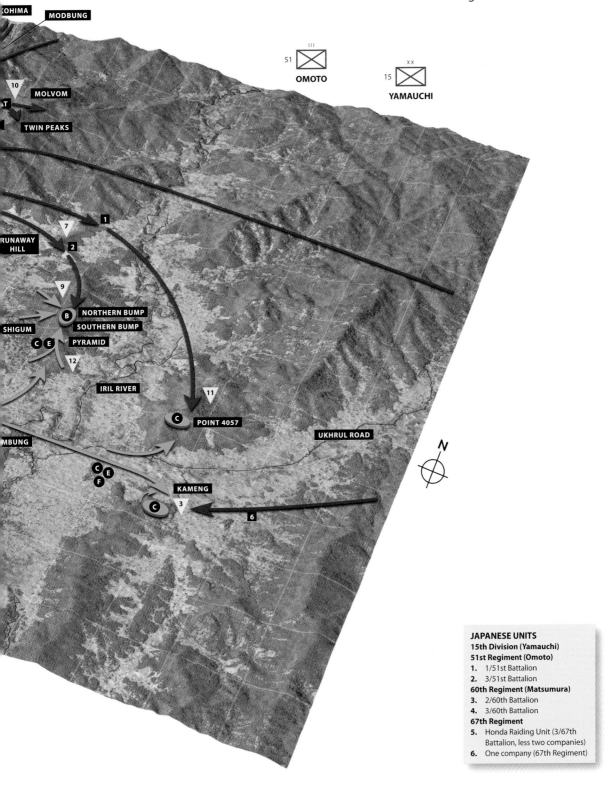

JAPANESE UNITS
15th Division (Yamauchi)
51st Regiment (Omoto)
1. 1/51st Battalion
2. 3/51st Battalion
60th Regiment (Matsumura)
3. 2/60th Battalion
4. 3/60th Battalion
67th Regiment
5. Honda Raiding Unit (3/67th
    Battalion, less two companies)
6. One company (67th Regiment)

Present-day view of the Ukhrul Road in the Imphal Valley as it approaches the hill (visible on the right) near Kameng that was attacked by the Japanese in early April 1944. (Author's collection)

Lion Box was similarly manned, with very few fighting troops among the several thousand men within its perimeter. The box was defended against mounting Japanese assaults from 4 to 7 April, while the evacuation of the supplies to Imphal continued apace. Its defence was assisted by units of the 9th Indian Brigade and tanks of the 3rd Carabiniers, who would travel up from Sekmai in the south during the day. Sekmai was also reinforced on 5 April by the 63rd Indian Brigade (17th Indian Division), which had just come up the Tiddim Road and was now to act as Corps reserve. Its arrival would soon release the 9th Indian Brigade to move eastwards towards Nungshigum.

With its defence becoming increasingly untenable, the evacuation of the box was finally ordered on 7 April. Sekmai now became the front-line British defensive position on the Imphal–Kohima Road. The defenders of Lion Box had allowed for the evacuation of a large amount of the most valuable supplies to Imphal. Yet again, Japanese hopes of easily securing bounties of supplies and rations abandoned by fleeing British forces were dashed.

To the east, the Japanese 51st Regiment (the centre column) had arrived in the hills around the village of Mapao at the end of March on schedule. En route, it had left a couple of units on the Saddle on the Ukhrul Road. The original plan was for this regiment to take Sekmai, as part of the attack on Imphal from the north, with the 60th Regiment to its west. But Yamauchi changed this, possibly because he wanted to bolster his forces on the Ukhrul Road and not spread his units too thin. He decided to move the main targets of both regiments eastwards: the 51st Regiment was to move towards the Nungshigum massif and its vicinity, while the 60th Regiment was to target Sekmai and the hills east of the Imphal–Kohima Road, including the Mapao–Molvom Range.

Yamauchi also aimed at the Ukhrul Road closer to Imphal in the first week of April. On 4 April, one company put in an attack against a feature near the village of Kameng, south of the road. This was where the road ran through a gap of just under a kilometre between two hill ranges, before it entered a more open stretch of paddy fields. It presented an easy approach route to Imphal. The 123rd Indian Brigade (5th Indian Division) had closed the gap with barbed wire and set up defensive positions in the hills to the immediate north and south of the road. It was the latter, held by the 1/17th Dogras, which came under attack.

The Japanese assault was held and they could not break into the position. They were then furiously counter-attacked by the guns of the 28th Field Regiment and by the Dogras themselves. A troop of tanks each of the 3rd Carabiniers and 7th Cavalry were also positioned on either side of the hill and fired on what were easy targets. By the next morning, almost 100 Japanese bodies were found; the few survivors had withdrawn. It is believed that the ultimate objective of this attack had been the fair-weather Kangla Airfield farther south.

While the immediate danger was averted at Kameng, an even greater threat to the airfield – and indeed to Imphal – was developing in the form of the Japanese 51st Regiment's move towards Nungshigum. The massif the British called Nungshigum had two high 'bumps' – northern and southern – on its central ridge, with spurs emanating in all directions. The Japanese knew it as Hill 3833, a reference to the height (in feet) of its highest point.

On 6 April, the Japanese first attacked a 3/9th Jat (9th Indian Brigade) standing patrol on a small hill to the north-west of Nungshigum. The position was lost. A few hours later, Jemadar Abdul Hafiz was tasked with recovering it with two sections of his platoon. He fearlessly led the way and recovered the feature in the face of a hail of machine-gun fire and grenade attacks, killing several Japanese in the process. Injured by now, Hafiz continued the attack, fought to his death and was posthumously awarded the Victoria Cross. The hill became known as Runaway Hill because of the way the Japanese had fled from Hafiz's brave actions.

But the battle at Runaway Hill was just the opening stage of the Japanese attack on Nungshigum. On 7 April, they attacked the massif and took its heights from two Jat platoons that had arrived there just a day earlier. In the four days that followed, Nungshigum exchanged hands a couple of times: the 3/9th Jats recovered it, only to lose it again to the Japanese (of the 3/51st Battalion) by 11 April. Now the Japanese dug in well on the northern and southern 'bumps'.

To the British, the Japanese presence at Nungshigum posed an unacceptable threat: IV Corps headquarters and Imphal Main were some 8km (five miles) away, while Kangla Airfield and the outskirts of Imphal were even closer. It was decided to evict them with all speed. Major-General Briggs, who commanded the 5th Indian Division, now brought massive firepower and resources and directed them at Nungshigum. This involved the infantry, artillery, air force and, amazingly (given Nungshigum's slope and height), armour. The main counter-attack was launched on 13 April, and it was recovered the same day (see Nungshigum artwork). The bold use of tanks sealed the fate of the Japanese here. Indeed, among the chief reasons for the 15th Division's ineffectiveness at Imphal was that it had not expected to encounter tanks.

Another battalion of the 51st Regiment attacked Point 4057 north of Kameng on the Ukhrul Road, but it was soon forced out to the hills to the north. Nungshigum was the closest the Japanese would come to Imphal in 1944. After the battle for this massif, Yamauchi's division would never be able to pose such an urgent threat from the north again. It attacked the 63rd Indian Brigade at Sekmai on the Imphal–Kohima Road on 13 April and then again some five days later, but both attacks were repulsed. On 19 April, the Japanese abandoned their effort to break through at Sekmai. And so by roughly mid-April, the Japanese advance had been stopped on the entire arc of mountains to the north of Imphal.

Present-day view from the east of the Nungshigum massif looming over the paddy fields and villages of the Imphal Valley. Medium tanks of the 3rd Carabiniers were sent up this feature, together with the infantry, to evict the Japanese from its heights in April 1944. (Author's collection)

THE BATTLE OF NUNGSHIGUM, 13 APRIL 1944 (PP. 44–45)

The massif the British called Nungshigum and the Japanese named Hill 3833 was the scene of an iconic battle. Its decisive day was 13 April 1944, when the 5th Indian Division directed a counter-attack to retake it from the Japanese. Involved in it were two companies of the 1/17th Dogra Regiment; the artillery of the 5th Indian Division, with another medium artillery regiment in support; the tanks of B Squadron, 3rd Carabiniers; and two squadrons of Vengeance dive-bombers and one of Hurribombers.

That morning, the infantry and tanks began climbing up via two spurs on the south-eastern side of Nungshigum. On each spur was a troop of M3 Lee/Grant tanks (1), together with a company of Dogras (2). The division's artillery, together with another troop of tanks, had been placed to the east and west of Nungshigum on the plain. As the infantry and armour climbed, the Vengeance dive-bombers and Hurricanes bombed and strafed the peaks (3). Soon thereafter, the artillery (some 88 guns in all) and tanks on the plain plastered the same area.

The two groups of infantry and tanks joined up at the peak named Pyramid and proceeded in a single file up a narrow ridge towards the Japanese on Southern Bump (4). As they approached the Japanese defences, fierce fighting erupted. The tanks were sprayed with machine-gun and rifle fire, and grenades were thrown at them. But there was only so much the Japanese could do. The use of armour on Nungshigum, which rose over 310m (1,000ft) above the valley floor, was a masterstroke. The Japanese had never expected to encounter tanks and they had nothing to counter them effectively.

The British had to pay a high price, too. All of the British tank officers were killed and the infantry officers wounded later that day. The former had been shot as they stuck their heads out of their tanks' turrets to guide them safely on the narrow and steep ridgeline. It was finally left to the VCO of the Dogras, Subadar Ranbir Singh, and Squadron Sergeant-Major Craddock of the 3rd Carabiniers to complete the battle. They rose to the occasion; the tanks finally destroyed the main bunkers and the infantry charged at and killed any survivors. There were casualties on both sides, but Japanese losses were especially heavy (250 bodies were later recovered). This was the closest the Japanese would come to Imphal as a large, organized force in 1944.

A BATTLE OF ATTRITION, MID-APRIL TO MAY 1944

Scoones had managed to concentrate the divisions under his command in and around the Imphal Valley by 4 April. About a fortnight later, the Japanese had been held on all of the spokes leading to the hub at Imphal. This gave way to a period of attrition when both sides faced each other in the hills and the valley in a gruelling test of will and stamina. The situation would roughly be as follows: on the Tiddim Road and the Silchar Track in the south-west would be the 17th Indian Division, along with the 32nd Indian Brigade (20th Indian Division). They would be up against the bulk of the Japanese 33rd Division. On the Tamu–Palel Road in the south-east, facing Yamamoto Force would be the 20th Indian Division. On and around the Ukhrul Road in the north-east would be the 23rd Indian Division, while to the north would be the 5th Indian Division and 7th Indian Division's 89th Indian Brigade (from early May). They would face the Japanese 15th Division. In mid-May, the 20th Indian Division and 23rd Indian Division switched places.

Through it all, and as had already become evident in the 5th Indian Division's arrival and Cowan's withdrawal from Tiddim, Fourteenth Army had an insurmountable and enduring advantage over the Japanese: support from the air. The Allied air forces and their personnel – including Britons, Americans, Indians, Canadians, Australians and New Zealanders – rendered yeoman service around Imphal. They flew in reinforcements just in time; brought supplies that sustained the besieged IV Corps ('*Stamina*' was the codename for the maintenance of the corps by air supply from 18 April to 30 June); evacuated casualties; and softened Japanese targets – among other sorties, all in very difficult flying conditions. The fighter squadrons maintained complete superiority over the Japanese in the skies above Imphal to ensure safety for the transport aircraft.

The related figures are impressive. Over the course of the battle, some 20,000 reinforcements were flown in, as were around 22,000 tons of supplies. Over 35,000 non-combatants and 10,000 casualties were flown out. One estimate for the total number of all kinds of Allied air sorties flown in support of Imphal and Kohima from March to July 1944 is a staggering 30,000; in comparison, the Japanese flew 1,750 sorties.

Members of the No. 1 Indian Air Force Squadron at Imphal, May 1944. (USI-CAFHR)

Imphal: hub and spokes

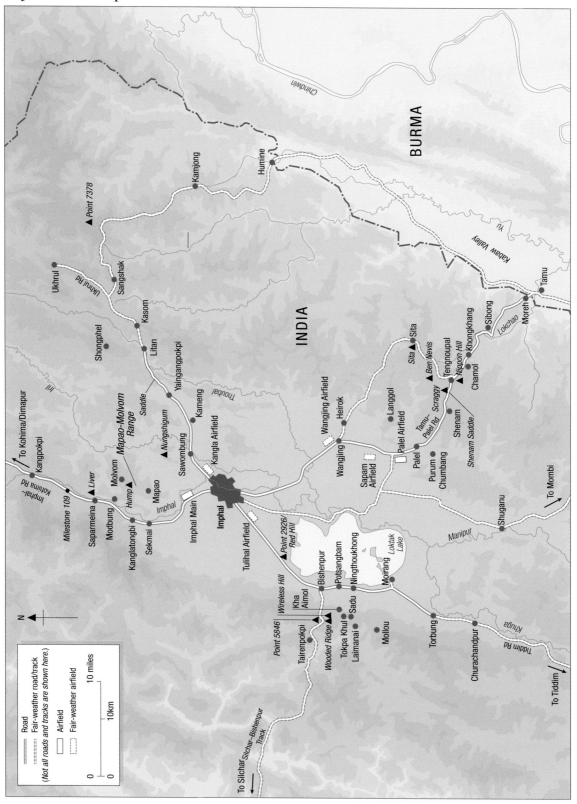

BURMA

INDIA

Chindwin

Kabaw Valley

Yu

Point 7378

Kamjong

Humine

Ukhrul

Ukhrul Rd

Sangshak

Shongphel

Kasom

Tamu

Litan

Sibong

Lokchao

Moreh

Khongkhang

Yaingangpokpi

Sita

Sita

Ben Nevis

Tengnoupal

Nippon Hill

Chamol

Mapao-Molvom Range

Saddle

Nungshigum

Kameng

Troubal

Wangjing Airfield

Heirok

Scraggy

Shenam

To Kohima/Dimapur

Kangpokpi

Sawombung

Kangla Airfield

Langgol

Palel Airfield

Tamu–
Palel Rd

Shenam Saddle

Imphal–
Kohima Rd

Liver

Molvom

Hump

Milestone 109

Saparmeina

Modbung

Mapao

Wangjing

Palel

Purum

Chumbang

To Mombi

Kanglatongbi

Sekmai

Imphal

Imphal Main

Sapam Airfield

Imphal

Point 2926/
Red Hill

Manipur

Shuganu

Tulihal Airfield

Bishenpur

Potsangbam

Ningthoukhong

Loktak Lake

Moirang

Wireless Hill

Kha
Aimol

Point 5846

Tairenpokpi

Wooded Ridge

Tokpa Khul

Sadu

Laimanai

Mollou

Torbung

Churachandpur

Tiddim Rd

Khuga

N

To Silchar

Silchar–Bishenpur Track

To Tiddim

Legend

Road
Fair-weather road/track
(Not all roads and tracks are shown here.)
Airfield
Fair-weather airfield

10 miles
10km

0
0

THE SOUTH-WEST

Having failed to prevent the withdrawal of the Black Cats (the 17th Indian Division, so called because of their divisional emblem of a black cat) from Tiddim, the White Tigers (a name used for the 33rd Division in reference to an old Japanese legend) now charted their own advance on Imphal. After moving up on the Tiddim Road, their main thrust was now made via the western hill range that skirted the Imphal Valley. Two columns, consisting of the 214th and 215th Regiments, had taken to the hills as the division reached the valley. Sakuma's 214th Regiment climbed up from near Churachandpur, while Sasahara's 215th Regiment moved up from near Moirang. Each was given separate targets. Sakuma was tasked with going north of the Silchar Track; his men would then descend back onto the valley to strike at Imphal. Sasahara's objective was the track itself; he was to try to deny its use to the British and secure a corridor through it to supply the 214th Regiment to the north.

A key target for both sides was the area where the Silchar Track crossed over the top of the western hill range. Point 5846 was a high peak north of where the road crossed, while Wooded Ridge and Wireless Hill were lower features to the south. Because they overlooked the road at its highest point as it crossed over, their capture was a priority.

And so in mid-April 1944, both sides raced for them: the Japanese northwards along the ridgeline, the British forces westwards from Bishenpur up the Silchar Track. The latter, in the form of the 7/10th Baluchis, were able to take Point 5846 just before the Japanese got there. The 214th Regiment immediately put in attacks on the peak, but were repulsed. The 32nd Indian Brigade went on to secure its position on Point 5846, which it retained right through to the end of the battle – with the 1st Battalion, the Northamptonshire Regiment, the primary defenders.

Present-day view of Point 5846 (locally known as Laimaton), the peak that dominated the Silchar Track as it crossed the western hills overlooking the Imphal Valley. The British beat the Japanese in the race to occupy this feature in mid-April 1944 and retained it through the battle. Two Victoria Crosses were won near here in June. (Author's collection)

The two sides struggled for Wooded Ridge and Wireless Hill. Hand-to-hand fighting ensued as each side sought to gain possession of these hills. The British had brought up a troop of Lee/Grant tanks of the 150th Regiment RAC (Royal Armoured Corps) from Bishenpur and these were pressed into battle, firing in close support of the infantry. By 26 April, Point 5846 and Wooded Ridge were under their firm control, while the Japanese had Wireless Hill. In the meantime, elements of the 214th Regiment had skirted Point 5846 from the west and reached north of the track.

The 215th Regiment made for the track itself. Once it leaves the valley, the Silchar Track starts climbing the western hills. On both sides was thick vegetation, which pressed in; it was so dense in places that visibility was down to just a few metres. Overlooking the track from the north on its climb up to the top of the range was a series of bluffs and heights which became targets for the Japanese. The 32nd Indian Brigade established a series of picquets there to protect the track and keep it open for use. Among them, Water Picquet stood out in importance as it covered a rare water source near the track.

Close-quarter fighting ensued. The Japanese put in repeated attacks and cut the track, blocking the flow of supplies from Bishenpur up to Point 5846. The 32nd Indian Brigade responded by counter-attacking from both sides: up from Bishenpur and down from Point 5846. In these actions the infantry again received excellent support both from armour and from the artillery firing from Bishenpur. The track was reopened and the Japanese were prevented from opening their own corridor to the north. Both sides suffered hundreds of casualties, with over 200 casualties for one battalion of the 32nd Indian Brigade alone.

Down on the Tiddim Road, a Japanese column had advanced parallel to those in the hills. This was formed around the 4th Independent Engineer Regiment, led by Colonel Taguchi, together with an infantry battalion

The battle for Bishenpur, 10–30 May 1944

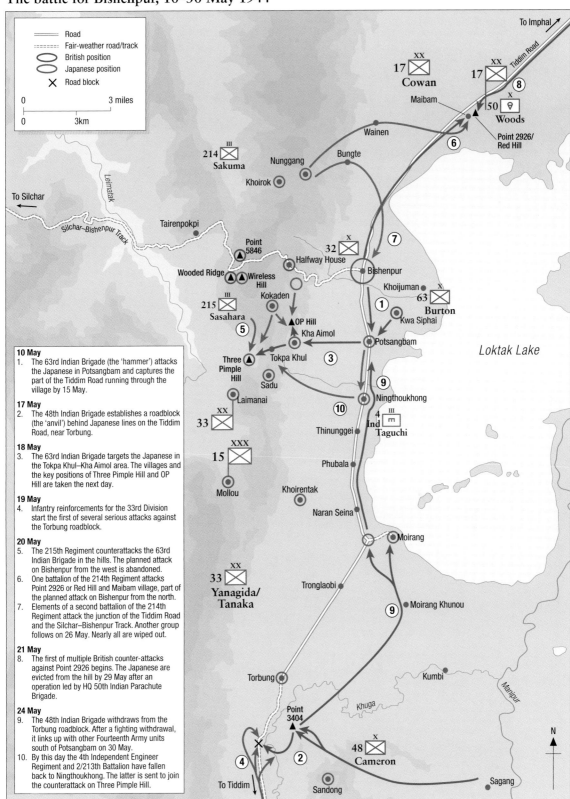

Legend:
- Road
- Fair-weather road/track
- British position
- Japanese position
- × Road block

0 — 3 miles
0 — 3km

To Imphal

17 XX Cowan

17 XX

50 × Woods

8

Maibam

Point 2926/
Red Hill

6

Wainen

Bungte

Nunggang

214 III Sakuma

Khoirok

7

To Silchar

Leimatak

Silchar–Bishenpur Track

Tairenpokpi

Point 5846

Halfway House

32 X

Bishenpur

Khoijuman

63 X Burton

Kwa Siphai

Wooded Ridge

Wireless Hill

Kokaden

215 III Sasahara

5

OP Hill

Kha Aimol

1

Potsangbam

Loktak Lake

Three Pimple Hill

Tokpa Khul

3

9

Ningthoukhong

4 Ind III Taguchi

Sadu

Laimanai

33 XX

10

Thinunggei

15 XXX

Phubala

Mollou

Khoirentak

Naran Seina

Moirang

33 XX Yanagida/Tanaka

Tronglaobi

9

Moirang Khunou

21 May

Torbung

Kumbi

Manipur

Point 3404

Khuga

4

2

48 X Cameron

N

To Tiddim

Sandong

Sagang

10 May
1. The 63rd Indian Brigade (the 'hammer') attacks the Japanese in Potsangbam and captures the part of the Tiddim Road running through the village by 15 May.

17 May
2. The 48th Indian Brigade establishes a roadblock (the 'anvil') behind Japanese lines on the Tiddim Road, near Torbung.

18 May
3. The 63rd Indian Brigade targets the Japanese in the Tokpa Khul–Kha Aimol area. The villages and the key positions of Three Pimple Hill and OP Hill are taken the next day.

19 May
4. Infantry reinforcements for the 33rd Division start the first of several serious attacks against the Torbung roadblock.

20 May
5. The 215th Regiment counterattacks the 63rd Indian Brigade in the hills. The planned attack on Bishenpur from the west is abandoned.
6. One battalion of the 214th Regiment attacks Point 2926 or Red Hill and Maibam village, part of the planned attack on Bishenpur from the north.
7. Elements of a second battalion of the 214th Regiment attack the junction of the Tiddim Road and the Silchar–Bishenpur Track. Another group follows on 26 May. Nearly all are wiped out.

21 May
8. The first of multiple British counter-attacks against Point 2926 begins. The Japanese are evicted from the hill by 29 May after an operation led by HQ 50th Indian Parachute Brigade.

24 May
9. The 48th Indian Brigade withdraws from the Torbung roadblock. After a fighting withdrawal, it links up with other Fourteenth Army units south of Potsangbam on 30 May.
10. By this day the 4th Independent Engineer Regiment and 2/213th Battalion have fallen back to Ningthoukhong. The latter is sent to join the counterattack on Three Pimple Hill.

51

Present-day view from the Silchar Track of villages and paddy fields around the Tiddim Road in the Imphal Valley, with Loktak Lake in the distance. (Author's collection)

A Hawker Hurricane Mark IIC of No. 42 Squadron RAF based at Kangla, piloted by Flying Officer 'Chowringhee' Campbell, diving to attack a bridge near a small settlement on the Tiddim Road. The bombs of the previous aircraft can be seen exploding on the target. (IWM, CF 175)

(2/213th Battalion) and an anti-tank gun detachment. They had arrived in Potsangbam, just over 3km (two miles) to the south of Bishenpur, in the second half of April.

The Japanese forayed into the villages of Kwa Siphai and Khoijuman to the north-east, but they were rebuffed. To counter them, aerial bombardments were called in on Potsangbam and the next large village, Ningthoukhong. Strategic Air Force Liberators pattern-bombed the two villages with 1,000lb bombs. The British sent tanks, together with infantry units, across the paddy fields towards Potsangbam, but their advance was held up by fierce opposition. Unlike at Nungshigum, the Japanese here were armed with anti-tank guns. Evicting them would require that much more effort.

The stretch of the Tiddim Road in the Imphal Valley provided a very different setting from the hills. For much of its length in the flat valley, the road ran through paddy fields. At regular intervals on the road were villages, with the fields filling the intervening distances. No wonder that the fighting in this area would come to be described by some British commanders as village and paddy field fighting. The terrain and layout of these villages themselves were quite distinctive. The residents' dwellings lay in compounds surrounded by fruit trees and bamboo clumps; the village itself was ringed by the latter. Small embankments and fish ponds were everywhere, with a stream often flowing through the village to the lake. It was all quite suitable for defence. Combine that with the Japanese, among the most tenacious and determined soldiers anywhere, and Fourteenth Army units had their work cut out.

The Japanese Army Air Force made four air raids on the Gun Box position in Bishenpur in the first ten days of May. There was good reason for this, for at Gun Box the 32nd Indian Brigade had concentrated its artillery support. This included four 3.7in. howitzers, eight 25-pdrs, six 6-pdrs and three A/A guns. From here the guns were able to support the infantry's actions both on and around the Silchar Track, as well as the villages on the Tiddim Road such as Potsangbam. The Japanese heavy field artillery was at Khoirentak.

The stage was now set for a crucial clash between the White Tigers and the Black Cats on this south-western approach to Imphal. May would be the decisive month. If the gravest threat to Imphal in April came from the north, in May it came from this direction. For the 33rd Division may have been bloodied in its failed mission to prevent the 17th Indian

Division's withdrawal, but it remained one of the most powerful divisions the Japanese had in Burma. Moreover, Imphal was still close; only Bishenpur stood in the way.

His original deadline missed, Mutaguchi also believed that the best chance his army still had of capturing Imphal was from the south-west. He became more personally involved in directing the 33rd Division's actions around Bishenpur at this time. From the end of May to the beginning of June, he had a command post in Mollou in the hills west of the Tiddim Road. Yanagida was on his way out. A Fifteenth Army order in mid-May relieved him of his command (effective some ten days later). He was to be replaced by Major-General Tanaka.

As May progressed, the commanders on both sides contemplated their next move. For the Japanese, a breakthrough at Bishenpur was the priority, especially before the monsoon set in later that month. If they could breach Cowan's defences here, they could march relatively unencumbered all the way to Imphal. Mutaguchi felt the way to do so would be a three-pronged attack on Bishenpur, involving a push up the Tiddim Road, an attack down from the Silchar Track area (by the 215th Regiment) and a strike from the north (by the 214th Regiment).

He also called for reinforcements, including an infantry regiment (the 151st Regiment, less one battalion) and another two infantry battalions. As an indicator of where Mutaguchi's priorities now lay, he ordered the move of the following from the Tamu–Palel Road to the Tiddim Road: the 14th Tank Regiment, 1st Anti-Tank Battalion and 2/18th Heavy Field Artillery Battalion.

Cowan also devised a plan to tackle the Japanese at the same time. This would entail a hammer and anvil approach: the hammer (63rd Indian Brigade) would be a push down from Bishenpur towards Potsangbam, Ningthoukhong and farther south, while the anvil (48th Indian Brigade)

Present-day view of the area of the Torbung roadblock of May 1944 (Tiddim Road). The hill in the background is Point 3404, which served as the base for the 48th Indian Brigade at the time. (Author's collection)

would be a roadblock on the Tiddim Road around Torbung, deep behind Japanese lines. He hoped the column of the Japanese 33rd Division on the road would be crushed between the hammer and anvil, while also cutting off the regiments in the hills. The fighting on this approach to Imphal in May resulted from the clash between these two opposing plans.

Consider the 17th Indian Division's strategy first. The part that went according to plan was the anvil. For this, Cowan had tasked the 48th Indian Brigade (Cameron) to march south of the Loktak Lake, secretly cross the Manipur River at Shuganu and establish a roadblock near Torbung. After a long and difficult march, the brigade group, including the 1/7th Gurkha Rifles and 2/5th Royal Gurkha Rifles, the 21st Indian Mountain Artillery and two mule companies, arrived near Torbung in mid-May. The roadblock was set up on 17 May where three nullahs crossed the road near Milestone 33. To the east were several low-lying hills where brigade headquarters was established, centred on one called Point 3404. The sluggish Khuga River flowed between the hills and the road.

For the next week, the roadblock was witness to intensive fighting. On the first night, eight lorries drove straight in and were destroyed. Two tanks were similarly dealt with. The Japanese reacted furiously to the discovery of the roadblock on their main supply line in the area. Over the next few days, several attacks were launched against it by the newly arrived infantry battalions (1/67th and 2/154th Battalions), while artillery fire was directed at both Point 3404 and the roadblock from the surrounding hills. Cameron's guns responded with retaliatory fire. The anvil of the roadblock held firm.

But Cameron was now informed that the hammer in the form of the 63rd Indian Brigade would not materialize. The 48th Indian Brigade would have to abandon the roadblock and head back. Faced with the choice of withdrawing along the route by which they had come or fighting through

Present-day view of the stream that runs through Potsangbam off the Tiddim Road. The Japanese and Fourteenth Army units clashed in the village and the banks of the stream in May 1944. By the 15th of that month, the 63rd Indian Brigade had secured the road through the village and the area of the stream to its east (visible here). (Author's collection)

to Bishenpur up the road, they chose the latter. By the time they left the roadblock on 24 May, it is estimated some 500 Japanese bodies had piled up in the vicinity. A week later, the brigade linked up with other British units near Potsangbam.

The Torbung roadblock had been a success for Cowan. Not only had it resulted in many Japanese casualties, it had also disrupted their supply line on the Tiddim Road at a crucial time. For this was when the Japanese were planning to launch a massive assault on Bishenpur. The roadblock had diverted their efforts for a week.

The hammer of Cowan's plan, the 63rd Indian Brigade (Burton), had been relieved from Sekmai in the first week of May by the 89th Indian Brigade. In its frustrated push southwards on the Tiddim Road, Burton had had to deal first with the determined Japanese defence of Potsangbam. He took over on 9 May from Mackenzie's 32nd Indian Brigade, which had gained a foothold in the village the day before and was now to give its full attention to the Silchar Track. The 63rd Indian Brigade put in a first attack on Potsangbam on 10 May. This involved two Gurkha battalions, each supported by a troop of tanks from the 3rd Carabiniers. The area they targeted was the main part of the village east of the Tiddim Road. The initial full frontal attacks failed to make much progress.

Burton then changed tack against the Japanese, who had withdrawn to their main defences south of the Potsangbam *turel*. He called for a heavy artillery bombardment from the same direction as before in the northern half of Potsangbam to make it appear that he was repeating the previous line of attack. Except this time he instructed one of his battalions to pass secretly behind the other and make for the area to the immediate east of the road. The move worked and the road through the village and its immediate vicinity were captured by 15 May.

The Tiddim Road through Potsangbam was now open, although the Japanese still held on in parts of the village. But it had all taken much longer than expected. While the anvil at Torbung was about to be put in place, the hammer had only inched forward. Cowan now decided to send the 63rd Indian Brigade to attack Japanese positions in the hills to the immediate west of the road – and then exploit south. He hoped that such a thrust would cut the supply line to the two Japanese regiments in the hills to the north, and force their withdrawal. The brigade set off on 18 May; the next day it had captured the villages of Tokpa Khul and Kha Aimol, and near them Three Pimple Hill and OP Hill respectively. But here again, the Japanese reaction was swift and dogged.

For the Japanese, all of these moves by the 17th Indian Division disrupted their planned assault on Bishenpur from the north, west and south at the exact same time. The Torbung roadblock had disrupted the movement of reinforcements and resources from the south. Now came Burton's incursion into the hills to the west, which put a spanner in the works for the planned attack from this direction. Mutaguchi reacted by abandoning the assaults from the west and south, and redirected the 215th Regiment to deal with Burton. All three of Sasahara's battalions were thrown into the counter-attack, the first of which went in on 20 May. Another major assault was made two days later; both were driven off. The Japanese lost over 110 men. But they persisted and put in further attacks over the next week, frustrating any further movement southwards for the 63rd Indian Brigade.

Burton's move into the hills also had other consequences. The Japanese abandoned Potsangbam, and by 24 May the 4th Independent Engineer Regiment and 2/213th Battalion had fallen back on Ningthoukhong. The latter was then sent to support the 215th Regiment's counter-attack on the Kha Aimol–Tokpa Khul area. Sasahara's counter-attack also allowed the 32nd Indian Brigade around Point 5846–Wooded Ridge finally to recapture Wireless Hill.

In the meantime, Mutaguchi had chosen to go ahead with only one part of his original plan to target Bishenpur: the attack from the north. He sent part of a battalion of the 214th Regiment to attack Bishenpur itself, while another was ordered to take Point 2926 (also known as Red Hill), a small hill off the Tiddim Road some 10km (six miles) north of Bishenpur. The latter attack was aimed at preventing the arrival of reinforcements from Imphal.

Both these assaults were pressed in on the night of 20–21 May. The one on Bishenpur targeted the area at the northern end of the village, near the junction between the Tiddim Road and the Silchar Track. Gun Box was near here. Once they had managed to infiltrate the road junction area, however, the Japanese were repeatedly counter-attacked in the next few days, British tanks firing on their positions at close range. Without any anti-tank guns, the unit was wiped out. The Japanese sent in another 70 men six days later, and they fared no better. The direct Japanese assault on Bishenpur is estimated to have cost the lives of some 360 of the 380 men of the 214th Regiment's first battalion.

The attack on Point 2926 farther north led to an even fiercer fight. The battalion of the 214th Regiment here had descended to the road from the western hills. They tried to storm Point 2926, but were beaten off by a platoon of the 7/10th Baluchs. Failing to take the peak, they captured the southern part of the feature and parts of the adjacent Maibam village.

Unbeknownst to the Japanese, Point 2926 had become quite important for the 17th Indian Division by this time, for the division's headquarters had recently been established just beyond it. An enemy force some 500 strong on the hill and in Maibam this close to headquarters was a threat that had to be dealt with urgently, but it did not prove an easy task. Reinforcements were rushed up from Bishenpur and Imphal, and three attempts were made to retake Point 2926 from 21–25 May. These did not succeed.

Present-day view of Point 2926 or Red Hill (locally known as Maibam Lotpaching) off the Tiddim Road, with Maibam village to its south. A site of a fierce battle at the end of May 1944, this was the closest any large Japanese force came to Imphal from the south. (Author's collection)

Indian Army soldiers manhandling boxes of ammunition on the Tamu–Palel Road, 1944. (NAM, No. 95986)

It was clear to Cowan that a much larger force was needed to evict the Japanese. This time a brigade-strength assault was planned. Executed by what became known as Woodforce, it involved the headquarters of the 50th Indian Parachute Brigade (commanded by Brigadier Woods) and was a composite force of tanks, artillery, sappers and infantry. Taking over the front on 26 May, Woodforce mounted robust counter-attacks over the next two days, finally overcoming all opposition and recapturing the hill and Maibam by 29 May. It is estimated that at the end of the battle the 500-strong Japanese force was reduced to some 40 soldiers. This was the closest an organized group of Japanese would come to Imphal from the south in 1944.

The failure of the Japanese assaults on and around Bishenpur weakened the 33rd Division considerably. Although the White Tigers still had some fight left in them, the last serious chance Fifteenth Army had of getting to Imphal had been lost.

THE SOUTH-EAST

By mid-April 1944, Yamamoto Force was back on Nippon Hill, the easternmost hill on the Shenam Saddle on the Tamu–Palel Road. The Japanese would now try to fight their way through the saddle. If they could get past this collection of hills, they could swoop down and take their first major target, the all-weather Palel Airfield, before heading to Imphal. The supply depots, dumps and other facilities in the Palel area also made it of special interest to the Japanese. It was equally imperative for Scoones and Gracey that Yamamoto Force be prevented from breaking through the Shenam Saddle. What followed was days of frenzied fighting on these beautiful but desolate hills at the highest point on the main south-eastern route into Imphal.

The capture of Nippon Hill on 16 April had handed an advantage to Yamamoto and would give much nuisance value. The hill offered clear views of some of the other features on the Shenam Saddle and the road below.

British movements could be observed from here and accurate firing from well-sited guns on this hill and the adjacent ridge caused many casualties among the defenders of the Shenam Saddle. The artillery support also came in handy as Yamamoto Force pushed forward.

By 22 April, less than a week after Nippon Hill had fallen one last time, the Japanese had overrun Crete East. Cyprus was left isolated and soon evacuated. The 80th Indian Brigade (Brigadier Greeves) had a difficult time. Unlike the other Japanese formations around Imphal at this point, Yamamoto's infantry could not only rely on solid assistance from artillery units, but they could also bank on the 14th Tank Regiment (before it was switched to the Tiddim Road later in May). The infantry charges here were thus well supported by both artillery and tank fire.

The Japanese pressed on. The next target was Crete West. Over the next two weeks, multiple attacks were directed at this hill. At one point, the Japanese managed to capture its lower reaches, but its defenders regained the lost ground. On 8 May, Yamamoto Force made for Lynch Pimple, the next hill. Lightly defended, it was captured easily. Now the units on Crete West were cut off from the rest of the 80th Indian Brigade: the hill could not be held for too long in such a situation and on 10 May it was evacuated. Scraggy became the easternmost British position on the Shenam Saddle.

Scraggy was first attacked late on the night of 10 May. The hill was extensively shelled, followed by a massive infantry assault: in classic style, wave upon wave of Japanese soldiers crashed on Scraggy, overwhelming its forward defences. Despite a spirited fightback, the attackers kept coming. A point was finally reached in the night when the British battalion commander on Scraggy felt that the hill would fall unless supporting artillery fire was directed on his own positions. This was called in and the Japanese advance finally halted on the morning of 11 May. But parts of Scraggy were now under the control of Yamamoto Force, which dug in. One veteran's account notes that Japanese casualties on Scraggy on that night alone were in the hundreds. They would remain on parts of Scraggy right until the end of the battle in July.

Soon thereafter, the 20th Indian Division exchanged places with the 23rd Indian Division. The exhausted defenders of the 80th Indian Brigade pulled out from the Shenam Saddle and made their way towards another front: the Ukhrul Road. The 37th Indian Brigade (Brigadier Collingridge) took over, its three Gurkha battalions – 3/3rd Gurkha Rifles, 3/10th Gurkha Rifles and 3/5th Royal Gurkha Rifles – supplemented by the 1st Seaforth Highlanders and 5/6th Rajputana Rifles in support.

The new arrivals were shocked to see the conditions on the forward positions of the Shenam Saddle. Scraggy stood out. The Japanese were on part of the hill, while the rest of it was under British control. Trenches and bunkers covered the feature; in places, mere metres separated the two sides' front trenches. Bits of body parts of soldiers lay everywhere and a terrible stench covered the hillside. Indeed, of all the sectors of the Imphal battle, it was the fighting on the Shenam Saddle – Scraggy in particular – that inspired comparisons with Kohima Ridge and even the Somme.

Gurkhas resting on Gibraltar on the Shenam Saddle in 1944. (NAM, No. 95985)

The Japanese attacks continued. On the night of 20–21 May, they rushed the crest of Scraggy in three waves, throwing gelignite bombs and grenades. They were beaten back. At the same time, they aimed for an even more ambitious target: Gibraltar, the most precipitous of the hills on the saddle. The main units involved here were from the two battalions (1/60th and 2/51st) of the 15th Division that had been attached to Yamamoto Force. Although their initial attacks were beaten off, the one on the night of 23 May succeeded and the Japanese gained possession of Gibraltar's crest. With the Fourteenth Army units on Malta and Scraggy cut off, the fate of the entire Shenam Saddle now hung in the balance, but the very next day the hill was recovered following a counter-attack led by the 5/6th Rajputana Rifles and 3/10th Gurkha Rifles. On the same day (24 May), Ben Nevis to the north was recaptured by the 1st Indian Brigade.

Gibraltar was the farthest the Japanese would be able to advance on the Shenam Saddle and the closest they came to breaking through. Meanwhile, they had again tried to bypass the saddle and the road from the north as well. After their setback at Sita in mid-April, they moved on and attacked Langgol village in the hills east of the Palel Airfield at the end of the month. There the advance was halted; the 48th Indian Brigade (17th Indian Division) deployed to deal with the incursion. Thereafter, the 1st Indian Brigade took over in clearing the hills north of the saddle.

At around the same time as this approach from the north, a 300-strong contingent also made an attempt via the hills from the south. But these were not Japanese: they were Indians of the INA's 1st Division. The first units of this division had arrived on the road in mid-April. The division's 2nd (Gandhi) Brigade was deployed on the left flank of Yamamoto Force and an initial group was rushed through the hills towards Palel. It was to try to target the airfield from the south in co-ordination with the Japanese closing in via Langgol from the east.

THE FIGHT FOR GIBRALTAR ON THE SHENAM SADDLE, 24 MAY 1944 (PP. 60–61)

Gibraltar, so-called after its namesake in the Mediterranean, was the steepest of the hills that made up the Shenam Saddle position on the Tamu–Palel Road. The Japanese knew it as Hill 5185, a reference to its height (in feet). The hill was witness to bitter fighting in May when Yamamoto Force attacked it as part of its attempts to push through these defences on the south-eastern approach to Imphal.

The initial attacks, including one on 20–21 May that lasted through the night, were beaten off. Another, more powerful attack came three days later, on 23 May. This time the Japanese were able to take parts of the hill, including its crest and the reverse slope. As daylight dawned on 24 May, the British, Gurkha and Indian units on the Shenam Saddle were shocked to see a Japanese flag fluttering on Gibraltar's peak **(1)**. This was dangerous: by taking this hill, the Japanese had isolated the positions on Malta and Scraggy. If their hold on Gibraltar was not broken, it would have made the defence of the other two hills untenable. The fate of the defences on the saddle hung in the balance.

Counter-attacks on Gibraltar were immediately ordered, starting with an artillery bombardment. One company of the 5/6th Rajputana Rifles, which still held part of the hill, then went in for the attack. It advanced up the narrow ridge leading to the crest, but had to withdraw after facing stiff resistance from the Japanese concentrated on the reverse slope. A company of the 3/10th Gurkha Rifles soon arrived as relief. The first of these Gurkhas **(2)** are seen here on the ridge and charging Gibraltar's crest in the face of grenade, machine-gun and rifle fire from the Japanese on the reverse slope **(3)**. Later that afternoon, fierce hand-to-hand fighting ensued and the Gurkhas captured the rest of Gibraltar. Some 145 Japanese bodies were later recovered.

The battle for Gibraltar typifies the sort of fighting that went on for months on the hills of the Shenam Saddle: positions exchanged hands as the two sides mounted a series of attacks and counter-attacks. A favourite Japanese tactic of situating themselves on the reverse slopes of hills is illustrated here, something they used to great effect in defending similar features around Imphal. Also highlighted here is the key role played by Indian and Gurkha units around Imphal to ensure a British victory in 1944.

In the end, the Japanese move had been foiled, but the INA's attack went through on the night of 2–3 May via the village of Purum Chumbang. There are differing accounts of what happened next. One has the INA group reaching very close to the airfield, while another has it reach some 8km (five miles) short of it. What is common to both, however, is the reaction of the Fourteenth Army units (Indian and Gurkha) to the INA's effort. A parley between the two is supposed to have taken place at some point, where the latter tried to convince their brethren on the British side not to fight. This being rejected, the INA attacked and was repulsed. At least 50 INA men were killed in the retaliatory response.

It has been argued that these attacks by their fellow Indians affected INA morale. They had not expected to be considered traitors by their former comrades of the Indian Army. Several hundred INA men deserted before the end of the battle, although the majority of the force remained in the hills around the Tamu–Palel Road, wracked by disease and hunger. The INA's 3rd (Azad) Brigade would arrive at the end of May and be deployed in the hills on the right flank of Yamamoto Force, while the main part of the 1st (Subhash) Brigade was sent beyond Ukhrul. But it would all be in support of a lost cause: the main Japanese thrust on this south-eastern approach to Imphal had failed by the end of May.

THE NORTH

Mutaguchi had not been happy about the 15th Division turning to the defensive north of Imphal after its last failed attack on Sekmai on 18/19 April. He instructed Sato (31st Division) in Kohima to send a regimental group down the Imphal–Kohima Road to Kanglatongbi to help Yamauchi resume offensive action. But the planned move was compromised by the capture of documents detailing it. Sato also realized he would not be able to do both at the same time – release a regimental group and hold Kohima – so he decided not to comply with Mutaguchi's order.

There was more bad news for Yamauchi. The 51st Regiment's (centre column) defeat at Nungshigum and subsequent withdrawal farther east had opened a gap between Colonel Omoto's men and those of the 60th Regiment and Honda Raiding Unit (right column). Instead of together posing a more potent threat to Imphal from the north, Yamauchi's two columns had been split apart. The right column was worst off. It was now much more isolated around the Imphal–Kohima Road and the Mapao–Molvom Range, its supply lines from the east under increasing threat from the 5th Indian Division. The only positive development for the 15th Division was in early May when it was reinforced by the arrival on the Ukhrul Road of 67th Regiment headquarters (its third regiment) and its last missing battalion (2/67th). But that was about it.

For the British, the Japanese thrust on Imphal from the north had been parried, but Yamauchi's division was still uncomfortably close by. Scoones' response in the northern front involved action against two broad areas to destroy the 15th Division. The 23rd Indian Division (Roberts) was made responsible for pushing back on the Ukhrul Road and regaining control of the Ukhrul area; the 5th Indian Division (Briggs) was tasked with clearing the Japanese from the Imphal–Kohima Road (up to Kangpokpi) and the Mapao–Molvom Range.

Roberts devised a two-pronged assault. The 37th Indian Brigade was instructed to advance up the Ukhrul Road, and the 1st Indian Brigade was sent on a wide flanking movement to the right, from where it was to swing north to try to capture Yamauchi's headquarters, believed to be in Kasom village in the hills near Litan. Both brigades made progress. The Saddle position above Yaingangpokpi on the road was captured and units of the 1st Indian Brigade entered Kasom, but Yamauchi's headquarters is thought to have moved farther north just as the brigade closed in.

By 22 April, both brigades had made contact on the Ukhrul Road near Litan. They then again set off on a chase of 15th Division headquarters, this time thought to be at Shongphel to the north. They converged on the spot, only to find Yamauchi was not there. A couple of weeks later, in mid-May, the 23rd Indian Division was withdrawn and moved to the Tamu–Palel Road. It switched places with the 20th Indian Division, which then resumed the drive against the Japanese on and around the Ukhrul Road.

Present-day view of the Ukhrul Road on its approach to Litan. First the 23rd Indian Division and then the 20th Indian Division fought northwards up this road in 1944 to recapture it from the Japanese 15th Division. (Author's collection)

Present-day view of the Mapao–Molvom Range in the distance (at the back) from the east. Visible here are the positions the British had named Twin Peaks (right of centre) and Hump (left of centre). The Japanese beat off at least half a dozen attempts to take the latter in May 1944 alone. (Author's collection)

Briggs and the 5th Indian Division faced a daunting prospect north of Imphal. There were no quick, dramatic victories to be won in peeling the Japanese back from their entrenched positions. Briggs initially concentrated his division's energies on the Mapao–Molvom Range. Its southern reaches practically overlooked IV Corps headquarters and Imphal Main. Now under the control of the 60th Regiment, these hills would prove among the toughest of nuts to crack. The Japanese dug in here would prove especially tenacious, resolutely clinging on to most of these positions. Unlike the Shenam Saddle and the Tamu–Palel Road, these peaks – with names such as Hump and Twin Peaks – could not be easily accessed by road. Any attempt to target them would involve climbing up the steep hillsides.

The two brigades of the 5th Indian Division got to work. Brigadier Salomons' 9th Indian Brigade attacked the Mapao–Molvom Range on 23 April, moving in from the east. His battalions had a hopeful start. After field guns had fired on and Hurricanes bombed Mapao, the 3/9th Jats and 3/14th Punjabis fought their way up and captured it two days later. But farther north, the heights around Molvom were better defended and the Japanese defied attempts to infiltrate these positions. The brigade soon got bogged down.

Meanwhile, the 123rd Indian Brigade (Evans) advanced up the Iril River Valley. It was to head north, before turning south-west towards Kanglatongbi and, in tandem with Salomons, crush the Japanese in between. It faced initial resistance in the hills to the east. These were occupied by the 51st Regiment, including the survivors of the battle at Nungshigum. After a week of fierce skirmishes, the 23rd Indian Division took over the task east of the Iril River as part of its push up the Ukhrul Road. This released Evans to continue his advance northwards up the valley, all along using every opportunity to disrupt Japanese supply lines.

The 9th Indian Brigade's attacks on the Mapao–Molvom Range failed to make much headway. Perhaps what best illustrated this punishing effort was the struggle for the peak named Hump. Hump was attacked by the brigade's battalions through the month of May. Heavy artillery and mortar fire and repeated air strikes were called in on it. The infantry also put in several attacks, suffering increasing casualties. Indeed, the men of the 3/14th Punjabis attacked Hump at least half a dozen times that month. Despite it all, the Japanese were still found in their bunkers at the end of May.

Men of the West Yorkshire Regiment clear a roadblock on the Imphal–Kohima Road. The 5th Indian Division led the drive to open this road northwards from Imphal. It entailed removing roadblocks such as these and evicting the Japanese from their positions in the hills alongside. (IWM, IND 3430)

Sited on the reverse slopes of Hump, their bunkers were difficult to target by guns firing from the other side. Even when they were hit, they were so solidly built that they suffered little damage. The defenders of Hump would wait until the 3/14th Punjabis neared the crest; they would then let loose a barrage of machine-gun fire and grenade attacks. Attack after attack had to be called off in the face of such furious resistance.

By mid-May, Briggs had decided to move the 123rd Indian Brigade to Sekmai to join the 89th Indian Brigade on the Imphal–Kohima Road. The difficulties on and around the road were twofold. The Japanese had set up roadblocks, but an even harder task was to deal with the Japanese in the hills along the road, where they had built bunkers and other defences. They could easily target the road from these positions. All of these needed to be tackled in order to open the road northwards from Imphal. Complicating matters further for long stretches here was the natural obstacle of the Imphal *turel* which flowed parallel to and between the road and the hills.

Briggs ordered the two brigades to start their advance: the 89th Indian Brigade was to target the hills to the east, while the 123rd Indian Brigade was to clear the roadblocks (starting 15 May). By 21 May, after about a week of fighting, both Kanglatongbi and the hills to the immediate east of the road between the village and Sekmai had been cleared. But this was just a few kilometres north of the starting point of Sekmai. Pushing back the Japanese was proving to be easier said than done.

As the month came to a close, Briggs decided to concentrate both his division's brigades on the Imphal–Kohima Road. The 9th Indian Brigade was to be brought on to the road, swapping places with the 89th Indian Brigade, which would move to the Iril River Valley. The opening of the Imphal–Kohima Road was a far greater priority than clearing the Mapao–Molvom Range. The Japanese defenders of the latter would be left where they had hung on for weeks. In any case, the opening of the road was likely to encourage them much more to leave than any direct attacks on their positions.

THE BRITISH BREAK THROUGH, JUNE 1944

By June, at all points of the compass around Manipur, the military advantage had slipped in favour of Fourteenth Army. Having stopped the Japanese advance on the main routes to Imphal and sparred with them through April and May, the Indian, Gurkha and British battalions were slowly beginning to make gains. But this was a painful exercise, as nowhere did the Japanese give up easily. Despite the odds and slim chances of success, the Japanese continued to launch attacks across Manipur. In fact, June 1944 saw some of the fiercest fighting between the two sides and four of the five Victoria Crosses at Imphal were won that month.

Not making things easier for either side was the weather. As it was, the two armies had been battling it out in difficult terrain and conditions. There were the steep and often jungle-covered hills, the heat for men not accustomed to it, the risk of tropical diseases like malaria and the leeches – not to mention the weeks and months of both physical and psychological strain from fighting a formidable enemy. The monsoon rains that began later in May only made matters worse.

As the days passed by, the low-lying areas in the Imphal Valley would flood because of the downpours, while the streams and small rivers everywhere would become raging torrents. The water level of Loktak Lake would also rise, making it especially uncomfortable for the units of both sides dug in at some of the lakeside villages on the Tiddim Road.

Dysentery and diarrhoea became an ever-greater concern. Foot rot would start to set in for men in their flooded positions. The slopes in the hills became slippery and that much more treacherous to navigate. The incessant rains would dissolve stretches of 'fair-weather' roads and 'jeepable' tracks into mud and slush everywhere, while triggering landslides in the hills. For the units on higher altitudes like the Shenam Saddle, Point 5846 and the Ukhrul area, the nights would become shockingly cold and damp, adding to their misery.

A unit of Bengal Sappers and Miners repairing a road near Tamu, 1944. The roads around Imphal needed constant maintenance and repair, but especially once the monsoon rains began. (NAM, No. 93888)

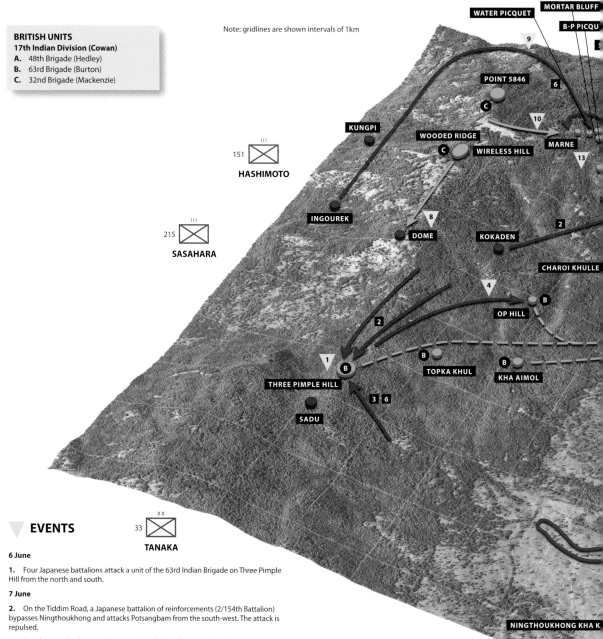

BRITISH UNITS
17th Indian Division (Cowan)
A. 48th Brigade (Hedley)
B. 63rd Brigade (Burton)
C. 32nd Brigade (Mackenzie)

Note: gridlines are shown intervals of 1km

WATER PICQUET MORTAR BLUFF
B-P PICQU

9

POINT 5846   6
C

KUNGPI   10
WOODED RIDGE   MARNE
C WIRELESS HILL   13

151 |X| III
HASHIMOTO

INGOUREK   8
215 |X| III   DOME   KOKADEN
SASAHARA

2
CHAROI KHULLE

4
B
OP HILL

2

B
TOPKA KHUL   B
THREE PIMPLE HILL KHA AIMOL

1
B

3 6
SADU

EVENTS

33 |X| XX
TANAKA

6 June

1. Four Japanese battalions attack a unit of the 63rd Indian Brigade on Three Pimple Hill from the north and south.

7 June

2. On the Tiddim Road, a Japanese battalion of reinforcements (2/154th Battalion) bypasses Ningthoukhong and attacks Potsangbam from the south-west. The attack is repulsed.

3. Simultaneously, the recently arrived 1/67th Battalion attacks North Ningthoukhong across the stream early on 7 June. A company attacks from the west. The attack fails and the Japanese pull out the next morning. For counter-attacking and defending his position to his death, Sergeant Hanson Victor Turner of the 1st West Yorkshires is posthumously awarded the Victoria Cross.

4. Two Japanese battalions (of the 215th Regiment) from the attack on Three Pimple Hill now target another unit of the 63rd Indian Brigade on OP Hill.

5. The 63rd Indian Brigade withdraws from Three Pimple Hill, OP Hill and the Tokpa Khul–Kha Aimol area later that night and marches towards Bishenpur.

12 June

6. The Japanese attack frontally over the stream again and capture a salient in North Ningthoukhong.

7. The lost ground in North Ningthoukhong is recovered in counter-attacks by units of the 48th Indian Brigade (including reinforcements sent from Potsangbam) later that day. Rifleman Ganju Lama (1/7th Gurkha Rifles) wins a Victoria Cross in this action.

13 June

8. After a first attempt to capture it was called off on the night of 10–11 June, the 32nd Indian Brigade puts in an attack on Dome on the night of 13–14 June. Japanese resistance is strong and the attack fails.

NINGTHOUKHONG KHA K

TO TIDDIM

21 June

9. The recently arrived Japanese 151st Regiment launches a wave of assaults against the British picquets north of the Silchar Track.

10. The 32nd Indian Brigade counter-attacks the Japanese in the picquets area from the west (from the Point 5846–Wooded Ridge–Wireless Hill area). Confused fighting rages for the next five days as positions are won and lost by both sides.

23 June

11. A unit of the 215th Regiment attacks and captures the picquet named Dog south of the Silchar Track.

25 June

12. Headquarters of the 48th Indian Brigade and a battalion (2/5 Royal Gurkha Rifles) are sent in as reinforcements from Bishenpur.

26 June

13. The Japanese capture Mortar Bluff early that morning. For defending the position to his death, Subedar Netra Bahadur Thapa of the 2/5th Royal Gurkha Rifles is posthumously awarded the Victoria Cross. Both Mortar Bluff and Water Picquet are retaken the same day. For his actions in recovering them, Naik Agan Singh Rai of the same unit wins the Victoria Cross.

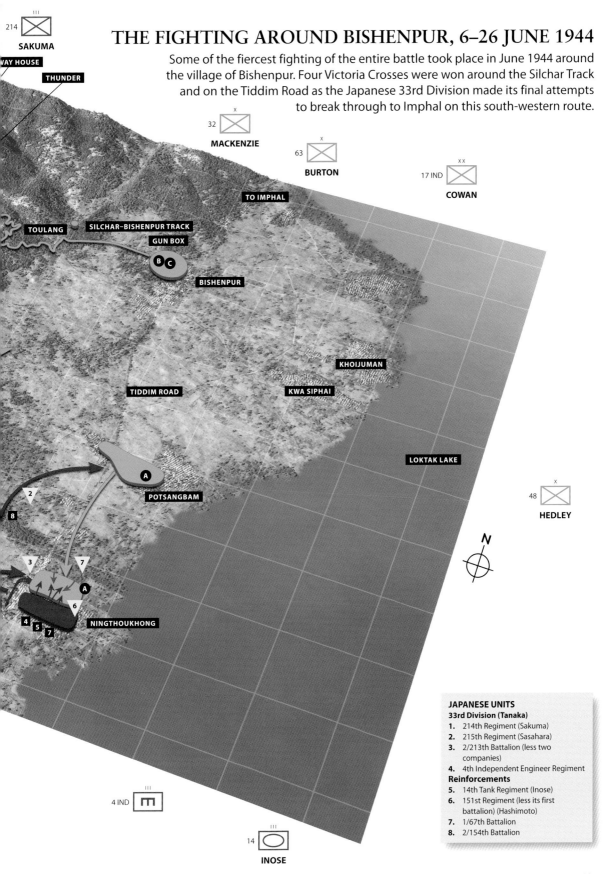

THE FIGHTING AROUND BISHENPUR, 6–26 JUNE 1944

Some of the fiercest fighting of the entire battle took place in June 1944 around the village of Bishenpur. Four Victoria Crosses were won around the Silchar Track and on the Tiddim Road as the Japanese 33rd Division made its final attempts to break through to Imphal on this south-western route.

214
SAKUMA

AY HOUSE

THUNDER

32
MACKENZIE

63
BURTON

17 IND
COWAN

TO IMPHAL

TOULANG

SILCHAR–BISHENPUR TRACK

GUN BOX

B C

BISHENPUR

KHOIJUMAN

TIDDIM ROAD

KWA SIPHAI

LOKTAK LAKE

48
HEDLEY

A

2

8

POTSANGBAM

N

3   7

A

6

4 5 7

NINGTHOUKHONG

JAPANESE UNITS
33rd Division (Tanaka)
1. 214th Regiment (Sakuma)
2. 215th Regiment (Sasahara)
3. 2/213th Battalion (less two companies)
4. 4th Independent Engineer Regiment
Reinforcements
5. 14th Tank Regiment (Inose)
6. 151st Regiment (less its first battalion) (Hashimoto)
7. 1/67th Battalion
8. 2/154th Battalion

4 IND

14
INOSE

But things were undoubtedly harder for the Japanese. They had carried few supplies and had not expected to be strung out fighting for so long. The rains and their impact on roads everywhere only compounded the, at best, inadequacy – at worst, absence – of supply arrangements. Most of the Japanese around Imphal were going hungry and many were wasting away from disease or injuries.

THE SOUTH-WEST

As in May, there was much fighting on the south-western approach to Imphal. The forceful Tanaka had replaced Yanagida at the 33rd Division headquarters in Laimanai (in the hills west of the Tiddim Road). Even though most of the surviving men in his exhausted division were worn out from weeks of campaigning, they had been bolstered by the arrival of infantry, armour (14th Tank Regiment) and heavy artillery reinforcements at the end of May. Tanaka now advanced his tactical headquarters to Sadu and urged the units under his command forward. He is famously said to have exhorted them to regard death as 'something lighter than a feather', claiming further that 'on this one battle rests the fate of the Empire'.

In the first week of June, the 63rd Indian Brigade's positions in the Tokpa Khul–Kha Aimol area were again targeted. This time around, four Japanese battalions were involved in the attack on Three Pimple Hill, of which two were redirected to OP Hill. All of the available Japanese guns in the area were instructed to fire on these features. In the face of this onslaught, Cowan finally decided to withdraw his brigade from the hills to Bishenpur on 7 June. Farther north, the 32nd Indian Brigade concentrated around Point 5846– Wooded Hill–Wireless Hill made two attempts to capture the feature called Dome from 10 to 14 June. While the first was called off, the second failed.

On the Tiddim Road, the focus of the fighting was again the villages and paddy fields to the south of Bishenpur. More than any other place, it was Ningthoukhong that was the fulcrum of the fighting between the two sides on the road in June. In terms of terrain and layout, the village was much like Potsangbam with its mix of houses, ponds, bunds, bamboo clumps and fruit trees. A *turel* also divided the village into northern and southern halves. Unlike Potsangbam, however, the Japanese had been in the village continuously since their arrival in April 1944. Initial attempts to dislodge them had proved unsuccessful. By June, the stream separated the two forces in the village east of the road; the 1st

Present-day view of Point 5846 and the hills skirting the western side of the Imphal Valley as seen from the Tiddim Road. A major part of the Japanese 33rd Division made its way and fought in these hills as it approached Imphal from the south-west. (Author's collection)

West Yorks, the 17th Indian Division's support battalion, had secured a part of North Ningthoukhong, while the Japanese were well entrenched in South Ningthoukhong.

The Japanese (4th Independent Engineer Regiment) at Ningthoukhong had been bolstered by the arrival of infantry and tanks as reinforcements. In line with Tanaka's exhortations, they now planned attacks both at Potsangbam and North Ningthoukhong. In the early hours of 7 June, the 2/154th Battalion bypassed Ningthoukhong and attacked Potsangbam from the south-west. It was repulsed, with the Japanese losing about 100 men.

A simultaneous attack was launched on North Ningthoukhong, led by the 1/67th Battalion. One company was to head out west from its stronghold, cross the stream and then turn back to attack the British positions in North Ningthoukhong (east of the road). They would be supported by light tanks. The rest of the battalion, supported by medium tanks, was to attack frontally. Manning the positions in North Ningthoukhong were the 1st West Yorks and two companies of the 2/5th Royal Gurkha Rifles.

The company's attack from the west was almost single-handedly held by Sergeant Hanson Victor Turner of the 1st West Yorks. Defending his platoon's position on the perimeter, Turner grabbed some grenades and charged forward, throwing them at the Japanese. He did this five times, going back to gather grenades each time and returning to the attack in the face of Japanese grenade and small-arms fire. He was killed on the sixth occasion while throwing a grenade. For his bravery, Turner was posthumously awarded the Victoria Cross. The Japanese eventually captured some ground in North Ningthoukhong, but withdrew after being struck from the air and shelled.

Five days later, on the morning of 12 June, the Japanese launched another big attack on North Ningthoukhong frontally across the *turel* (see Ningthoukhong artwork) and captured a salient on the other side. They were evicted later the same day, however, in a counter-attack in which Rifleman Ganju Lama of the 1/7th Gurkhas won a Victoria Cross.

JAPANESE ATTACK IN NINGTHOUKHONG, 12 JUNE 1944 (PP. 72–73)

Ningthoukhong on the Tiddim Road was the village that saw the most fighting between the Japanese and British forces in the Imphal Valley in 1944. The Japanese entered the village in April and would retain a presence there until their withdrawal in July.

Like other villages in the valley, such as Potsangbam, Ningthoukhong had a profusion of large bamboo clumps and fruit trees **(1)**. These grew everywhere, bunching up around the houses and their attached ponds, and ringing the villages themselves. Finding cover was easy and the Japanese were adept at using the vegetation and terrain to their advantage. Another distinctive feature – again like in Potsangbam – was the stream (or *turel*) **(2)** that flowed through to Loktak Lake, dividing the village into northern and southern halves. Narrow and muddy, with steep banks in parts, the stream ended up forming a natural barrier between the two sides: the Japanese had dug in to its south, while Fourteenth Army units were in the northern half of Ningthoukhong.

In June 1944, the Japanese 33rd Division made its last serious effort to try to break through on this approach to Imphal. Two major attacks (on 7 and 12 June) were launched from South Ningthoukhong on the British positions north of the stream. The manner in which they unfolded – as infantry and armour assaults, supported by artillery fire – mirrored many of Fourteenth Army's own operations in the area. A Victoria Cross each was won following both attacks.

On 12 June, an intense mortar and artillery bombardment, as well as tank fire, preceded the frontal Japanese infantry assault over the stream. The infantry had in support at least one light and four medium tanks firing at point-blank range. Here the Japanese infantry **(3)**, together with two medium tanks **(4)**, are seen crossing the stream as part of their assault. The thick foliage south of the stream provided them with good cover before the attack.

Across the stream, the Japanese were able to capture a salient some 185m deep by 275m wide (200 yards by 300 yards). Two of the tanks were put out of action by an anti-tank gun unit, while three got bogged down in the mud, a common problem for armour with the monsoon rains making these villages slushy and muddy. Later that afternoon, a counter-attack was ordered, led by two companies of the 1/7th Gurkha Rifles. Rifleman Ganju Lama won a Victoria Cross that day when, in the face of enemy fire and despite injuries, he single-handedly knocked out two of the bogged-down Japanese medium tanks with a PIAT and killed their crews. The Japanese were pushed back over the stream again later that day. This was the last of the major Japanese attacks on the Tiddim Road in 1944.

These were the last major attempts by the Japanese to break through to Bishenpur on the Tiddim Road in June. But they had still not finished trying, and now targeted the hills to the west. From 21 to 26 June, the newly arrived Japanese 151st Regiment (less one battalion) attacked the British picquets overlooking the Silchar Track. Water Picquet fell on 21 June. The Japanese had skirted around the west of Point 5846 and closed in on the position from the north. Intense assaults followed on all of the other picquets from the same direction. Some of the positions were won and lost in vicious hand-to-hand fighting. To help Mackenzie deal with this new offensive, the 48th Indian Brigade's headquarters and the 2/5th Royal Gurkha Rifles were among the reinforcements rushed up from Bishenpur.

On the night of 25 June, no less than a company of Japanese began attacking Mortar Bluff, a picquet position bereft of cover and a short distance away from Water Picquet. It was held by a small garrison of some 40-odd men of the 2/5th Royal Gurkha Rifles who had replaced the 7/10th Baluchis. In pouring rain, the Japanese first bombarded the position with mortars and guns at point-blank range. For the next few hours, the infantry repeatedly attacked the surrounded and dwindling garrison. Subedar Netra Bahadur Thapa defended the besieged position almost through the night, organizing counter-attacks with whatever ammunition and grenades his unit had left. The Japanese finally overran Mortar Bluff the next morning, with Netra Bahadur Thapa fighting to his death. He was posthumously awarded the Victoria Cross.

Present-day view of the old Silchar Track near Point 5846. Also locally known as the Old Cachar Road or Tongjei Maril, the Japanese and British forces fought for control of this track and its surrounding heights, especially the stretch from Bishenpur to Point 5846. (Author's collection)

A few hours later, a company of the same unit formed for a counter-attack on Mortar Bluff. In the face of heavy fire, Naik Agan Singh Rai led his section in charging a Japanese machine-gun post and killing its crew. It then recaptured Mortar Bluff and neutralized a 37mm gun position and crew. Rai now advanced on a Japanese bunker and killed its occupants, after which his company also recovered Water Picquet. For his actions that day, Rai won the Victoria Cross, the second for the 2/5th Royal Gurkha Rifles the same day. Faced with such counter-attacks and intense artillery fire from Gun Box, the last throw of the Japanese 33rd Division around the Silchar Track ended in failure.

THE SOUTH-EAST

After the Japanese had been evicted from Gibraltar on 24 May, they did not follow up with another major attempt to push through the Shenam Saddle for a fortnight. But there was never really a quiet moment on these heights. Sniper fire was ever-present, as was the booming of artillery guns. The situation was the worst on Scraggy, where both sides continued to maintain their respective positions. The British and Indian units here would be fired on from Nippon Hill, besides being subjected to rifle fire, mortaring and grenade attacks from Scraggy itself.

On the evening of 9 June, the Japanese put in their last major attack on Scraggy, starting with a heavy artillery bombardment. They next stormed the crest of Scraggy and captured it, its defenders (3/3rd Gurkha Rifles) having to fall back. Initial counter-attacks being driven off, a more powerful effort was made the next afternoon. Artillery concentrations were directed at the Japanese and an airstrike was made on their part of Scraggy and Lynch. The Gurkhas followed up with an advance. Although some ground was recovered, the Japanese maintained their grip on Scraggy's crest. Casualties on the British side had been high (one estimate puts the figure at 200) and no further attempts were made; it was also felt that the Gurkhas' new position was sufficiently strong. And so the Japanese were left where they were. They would remain in place until the end of July.

North of the Tamu–Palel Road, Yamamoto Force again tried to approach Palel Airfield in the second half of June. This involved the headquarters of the 213th Regiment, together with survivors of the previous attempts to attack from this direction. The Japanese managed to get beyond Langgol and attack some positions in the foothills near Palel Airfield, but were soon rebuffed. They finally sent in a commando raid on the airfield in early July, which succeeded in

A Japanese position under fire on the Tamu–Palel Road. (IWM, IND 3331)

blowing up eight planes. This proved that, even when Fifteenth Army was on its last legs, it remained a tough foe. Fourteenth Army could never afford to lower its vigilance on any of the approaches to Imphal.

THE NORTH

After its arrival on the Ukhrul Road in the second half of May, it became the responsibility of Gracey and his 20th Indian Division to figure out how best to tackle the Japanese 15th Division in the area. In early June, he sent the 80th Indian Brigade northwards from Kameng up the Iril River Valley. It was to go on a wide encircling move and come back down on the Ukhrul Road near Litan, targeting and clearing the Japanese positions encountered in the area. Resistance here was not too strong and the brigade made progress.

In comparison, the 100th Indian Brigade's (the division's second brigade) simultaneous advance on the Ukhrul Road was much hampered. It faced surprisingly fierce attacks on and around the Saddle position by the Japanese 67th Regiment, with artillery support (the remainder of the 15th Division's artillery had since arrived), and in the hills to the north by the 51st Regiment. Although the Japanese managed to gain some ground in this last-ditch effort, its main attacks on the road were repulsed and the 100th Indian Brigade consolidated its position on Saddle by mid-June.

Present-day view westwards of the Imphal Valley from the old Saddle position on the Ukhrul Road. In the distance are the villages of Yaingangpokpi and Kameng. (Author's collection)

But all eyes in June were on the fighting on the Imphal–Kohima Road, for the stakes here were much higher for both sides now. As the battle at Kohima wound down, opening the road between Imphal and Kohima became a primary objective for Fourteenth Army. There had also been growing concerns that the monsoon rains and related bad weather could affect the maintenance of IV Corps by air supply. Rationing was in place during the siege and had been intensified as it wore on. The siege of Imphal had to be lifted.

The task was comparatively easy for the British 2nd Division as it rushed down the road from Kohima. The Japanese here were on the back foot and resistance put up at places like Visvema and Maram was swiftly dealt with. The challenge was greater for the 5th Indian Division battling northwards up the road from Imphal (its 9th Indian Brigade had replaced the 89th Indian Brigade at the beginning of June). As a point of comparison, from 3 to 22 June, the British 2nd Division advanced some 95km (60 miles) southwards on the road, while the 5th Indian Division was able to move under 11km (seven miles) northwards.

The defenders of the 15th Division which the latter faced were aware that they were preventing the reopening of this vital supply line overland from Imphal. Once the road was opened, for all practical purposes, the Japanese offensive was over. These units (60th Regiment, Honda Raiding Unit), as well as those of the 51st Regiment, had in the meantime been suffering tremendously. Their supply lines to the east had been cut and no supplies were being received from the rear echelons.

The 5th Indian Division's two brigades – the 9th and 123rd Indian Brigades – pushed on. This involved a series of actions by the Indian and British infantry battalions to clear every Japanese roadblock on the road and position in the hills alongside. Each action required close artillery and armoured support, and often the calling in of air strikes. Their advance was

Present-day view of the feature named Liver and its vicinity near Saparmeina along the Imphal–Kohima Road. The Japanese here held up the 5th Indian Division's final push up the Imphal–Kohima Road by almost a week in June 1944. Also visible in the foreground is the Imphal *turel* (river). (Author's collection)

Opening of the Imphal–Kohima Road by the 5th Indian Division, 3–22 June 1944

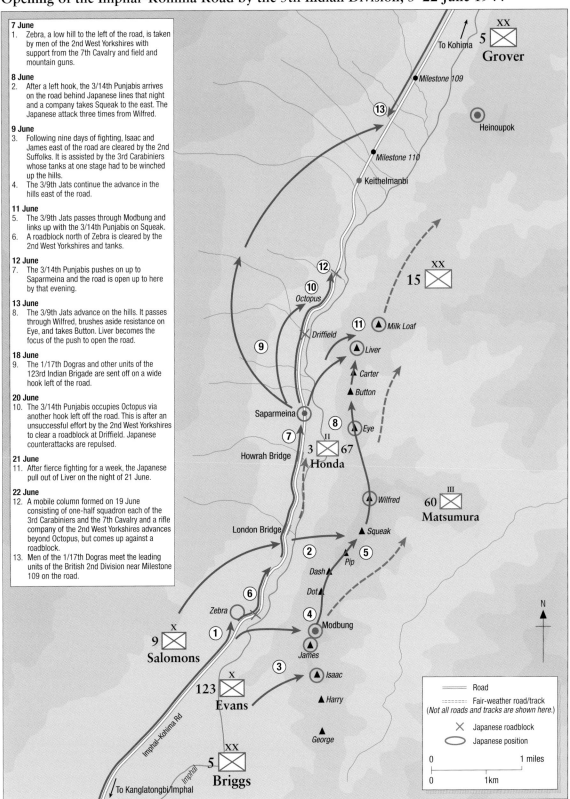

7 June
1. Zebra, a low hill to the left of the road, is taken by men of the 2nd West Yorkshires with support from the 7th Cavalry and field and mountain guns.

8 June
2. After a left hook, the 3/14th Punjabis arrives on the road behind Japanese lines that night and a company takes Squeak to the east. The Japanese attack three times from Wilfred.

9 June
3. Following nine days of fighting, Isaac and James east of the road are cleared by the 2nd Suffolks. It is assisted by the 3rd Carabiniers whose tanks at one stage had to be winched up the hills.
4. The 3/9th Jats continue the advance in the hills east of the road.

11 June
5. The 3/9th Jats passes through Modbung and links up with the 3/14th Punjabis on Squeak.
6. A roadblock north of Zebra is cleared by the 2nd West Yorkshires and tanks.

12 June
7. The 3/14th Punjabis pushes on up to Saparmeina and the road is open up to here by that evening.

13 June
8. The 3/9th Jats advance on the hills. It passes through Wilfred, brushes aside resistance on Eye, and takes Button. Liver becomes the focus of the push to open the road.

18 June
9. The 1/17th Dogras and other units of the 123rd Indian Brigade are sent off on a wide hook left of the road.

20 June
10. The 3/14th Punjabis occupies Octopus via another hook left off the road. This is after an unsuccessful effort by the 2nd West Yorkshires to clear a roadblock at Driffield. Japanese counterattacks are repulsed.

21 June
11. After fierce fighting for a week, the Japanese pull out of Liver on the night of 21 June.

22 June
12. A mobile column formed on 19 June consisting of one-half squadron each of the 3rd Carabiniers and the 7th Cavalry and a rifle company of the 2nd West Yorkshires advances beyond Octopus, but comes up against a roadblock.
13. Men of the 1/17th Dogras meet the leading units of the British 2nd Division near Milestone 109 on the road.

Road

Fair-weather road/track
(Not all roads and tracks are shown here.)

✕ Japanese roadblock

⬭ Japanese position

0 ——————— 1 miles

0 ——————— 1km

To Kohima

5 ⊠ Grover

● Milestone 109

● Heinoupok

● Milestone 110

● Keithelmanbi

15 ⊠

Octopus

Milk Loaf

Driffield

Liver

Carter

Button

Saparmeina

Eye

3 ⊠ 67
Honda

Howrah Bridge

Wilfred

60 ⊠ Matsumura

London Bridge

Squeak

Pip

Dash

Dot

Zebra

Modbung

9 ⊠ Salomons

James

123 ⊠ Evans

Isaac

Harry

5 ⊠ Briggs

George

Imphal–Kohima Rd

Imphal

To Kanglatongbi/Imphal

N

The link-up at Milestone 109 between units of the British 2nd Division fighting southwards from Kohima and the 5th Indian Division fighting northwards from Imphal on 22 June 1944. This ended the siege of Imphal. (IWM, IND 3495)

stubbornly resisted by the Japanese, who had been in the area for months. The 5th Indian Division also had to battle the elements: the monsoon was at its peak, the Imphal *turel* became a raging river, difficult to cross, and low-lying mists descended, making an already grim landscape even gloomier.

By 13 June, the division had progressed up to Saparmeina (sometimes called Safarmaina in war records), both on the road and in the hills alongside. Its final advance northwards rested on clearing the area around this village. The struggle over the next week centred on the main feature east of the road, the hill named Liver. The 3/9th Jats attacked repeatedly to try to dislodge the Japanese from this feature. One such attempt was made on 15 June, when Hurribombers strafed the hill, followed by heavy artillery concentrations from 25-pdrs, 3.7in. howitzers and 3in. mortars. A Jat company climbed the hill, but had to withdraw some 100 metres from its objective because of heavy machine-gun fire.

The last attempt was made on 21 June. Again, the Japanese positions were bombed and strafed from the air, this time by three squadrons of Hurribombers for half an hour. The 4th and 28th Field Regiments, as well as a troop of the 8th Medium Regiment, fired a concentration on Liver that covered it in dust and smoke. Three companies of the Jats now went in, and yet this attack was also held by the Japanese on and around Liver. They had had enough, however, and by the next morning were found to have withdrawn from the feature. The Jats suffered around 150 casualties that week, including 33 killed.

Meanwhile, the 1/17th Dogras, who had taken a wide left hook through the jungle, arrived near Milestone 109 on the road. On 22 June, they met up with men of the British 2nd Division coming down the road from Kohima. The Imphal–Kohima Road was now open. As Slim was to note later, the opening of the road meant that what he called the first decisive battle of the Burma Campaign was not yet over, but it had been won.

Present-day view of the area near the old Milestone 109 on the Imphal–Kohima Road where the two arms of Fourteenth Army met and lifted the siege of Imphal on 22 June 1944. (Author's collection)

A JAPANESE ROUT, JULY 1944

Whereas at Kohima the fighting had largely ceased by early June, it was not so around Imphal, where it would continue for at least another six weeks. Even after the Imphal–Kohima Road was opened on 22 June and supplies came through overland, the Japanese Fifteenth Army would put up resistance around Imphal throughout July. But now its exhausted units would have to face the combined strength of both IV Corps and the recently arrived XXXIII Corps from Kohima.

The initial dividing line between IV Corps and XXXIII Corps was an east–west one, making XXXIII Corps responsible for areas north of Imphal, including Ukhrul. After the recapture of Ukhrul, the line was made a north–south one, running from Kohima–Imphal–Palel. Then XXXIII Corps was given responsibility for the Shenam Saddle and the Tamu–Palel Road, while IV Corps was tasked with clearing the Japanese from the Silchar Track and the Tiddim Road.

On his part, Mutaguchi wrestled with the question of when to accept the inevitable and order the withdrawal of Fifteenth Army from around Imphal. The 31st Division had already withdrawn from the Kohima area in June,

General Stopford (right), Commander of XXXIII Corps, confers with Major-General Grover (left), GOC British 2nd Division, and Brigadier Salomons (centre) of the 9th Indian Brigade (5th Indian Division) after the opening of the Imphal–Kohima road. (Getty Images, No. 3038198)

Discarded Japanese equipment seen on Scraggy after it was recaptured at the end of July 1944. Visible in the distance on the right is Malta, and on the left is Gibraltar. (NAM, No. 95980)

Sato taking the decision unilaterally. Mutaguchi tried to involve Sato's division in a renewed push towards Imphal, but to no avail. In fact, Mutaguchi had had the opportunity in early June to call off the offensive in a meeting with Burma Army Commander Kawabe. It was already evident to both men that it had failed, and yet neither could get himself (or the other) to raise or admit this. Mutaguchi finally recommended the withdrawal of his army to Kawabe in the last week of June. This was passed up the chain of command for authorization. On 5 July, Kawabe ordered Mutaguchi to prepare to withdraw, but at the same time he told him to continue with his plan for an offensive on Palel.

The latter was a reference to – incredibly – a final throw by his army that Mutaguchi had been plotting: a combined attack on the Palel area by the 15th Division, the remnants of 31st Division and some units of 33rd Division. He issued an attack order, but his battered divisions were in no real position to comply. It was only on 9 July that Kawabe gave the final order to withdraw; Mutaguchi subsequently ordered his divisions to commence a phased withdrawal on 16 July. By this time, Ukhrul had already fallen. Yamamoto Force was asked to hold on to the Shenam Saddle for a little longer to allow for the retreat from the Kabaw Valley. By the end of the month, having been cleared from their last strongholds – considered below – and routed on all the approaches to Imphal, the Japanese were in full retreat towards the Chindwin.

The local bazaar at Imphal during World War II. The people of Manipur were much affected by the war in general and the Imphal battle in particular. During the battle, some locals supported the British, while others sided with the Japanese and the INA. (IWM, COL 218)

A final point is in order here about the natives of Manipur in relation to the Imphal battle. For places such as Ningthoukhong, Kanglatongbi and Ukhrul were not just points on the map or battlefields between the British and the Japanese forces. They were the homes and lands of the people of Manipur, who found themselves caught up in some of the bitterest fighting of World War II – from no fault of their own. During the war, the population of Manipur was around 512,000, of whom some 343,000 lived in the Imphal Valley and the rest in the hills. The majority ethnic group in Manipur were the predominantly Hindu Meiteis, who were concentrated in the Imphal Valley; the Christian Nagas and Kukis were the largest of the tribes in the hills.

While the majority of the local population tried to get by as normally as possible amid massive displacement caused by the fighting and the presence of over a couple of hundred thousand troops, others played a role in supporting the warring sides. In Kohima, the situation was fairly clear cut, with the Nagas extending their support to the British. Around Imphal, the response of the natives was more mixed. The Maharaja of Manipur, Bodhchandra Singh, and his Durbar backed the British. Then there were a couple of thousand men from the tribes in the hills who, as part of V Force, had been tasked with gathering intelligence about the Japanese and their movements.

But there were people from the different major communities in Manipur who also supported the Japanese and the INA. This was especially the case among the Kukis. For instance, many Kukis in the hills around the Tiddim Road assisted the INA; several even defected from V Force. Similarly, some Meiteis around Moirang helped the INA. Pro-Japanese sentiment was much less among the Nagas (Tangkhuls). In many cases, the response of the locals owed simply to where they were at the time of the fighting, and whom they had to deal with in order to survive the battle.

THE SOUTH-WEST

After their failed attempt on the picquets around the Silchar Track in June, the Japanese in the hills west of the Tiddim Road were slowly falling back. The 214th Regiment had been instructed to withdraw from north of Point 5846 to south of the Silchar Track in the first week of July. They were then ordered to proceed towards Laimanai, descend to the Tiddim Road and retreat southwards down the road. Other units in the hills, including the remnants of the 215th and 151st Regiments, were to follow the same route. Covering this general withdrawal from the hills was the Japanese force at Ningthoukhong and Ningthoukhong Kha Khunou on the Tiddim Road. This included the remnants of the 4th Independent Engineer Regiment, at least one infantry battalion (2/154th Battalion) and the last few remaining tanks of the 14th Tank Regiment. They were told to hold fast until the men in the hills had descended to the road behind them and moved south.

The 17th Indian Division was tasked with clearing the Japanese from south of the Silchar Track and evicting them from their last stronghold on the road in the Imphal Valley. Its 63rd Indian Brigade headed to the hills in the direction of Laimanai, while the 48th Indian Brigade moved in on Ningthoukhong (the 32nd Indian Brigade reverted to its parent 20th Indian Division). Progress was slow, even at this late stage of the battle, especially in the Ningthoukhong area.

The Maharaja of Manipur, H. H. Bodhchandra Singh, visits an Indian Air Force squadron at Imphal. He looks on with interest at the armament of a Hurricane. With him are Air Commodore S. F. Vincent of 221 Group RAF, Wing Commander P. H. Lee and Squadron Leader Arjan Singh. (USI-CAFHR)

By the middle of July, Japanese resistance centred on Ningthoukhong Kha Khunou. A small hamlet about 300 metres wide and 500 metres long, it lay to the immediate south of Ningthoukhong. Despite probing attacks by the 48th Indian Brigade's infantry and artillery firing on their defences, the Japanese held on. Finally, in the early hours of 16 July, this small space was subjected to what some describe as one of the heaviest artillery concentrations yet in the Burma Campaign; in the space of an hour, approximately 9,000 shells were fired on Ningthoukhong Kha Khunou. Fortunately for the Japanese, they had withdrawn from the village just before the shelling began. By the time it ended, the village had been completely flattened and was pockmarked with waterlogged craters.

And so the last Japanese stronghold in the Imphal Valley was taken. The 63rd Indian Brigade also reached and occupied the Laimanai area around the same time. The 5th Indian Division, the other division in the reconstituted IV Corps, now took over and commenced the chase of the Japanese 33rd Division down the road towards Tiddim.

The remains of Japanese dead, equipment and caved-in bunkers on Scraggy at the end of July 1944. (IWM, IND 3714)

Clearing the last Japanese strongholds around Imphal, July 1944

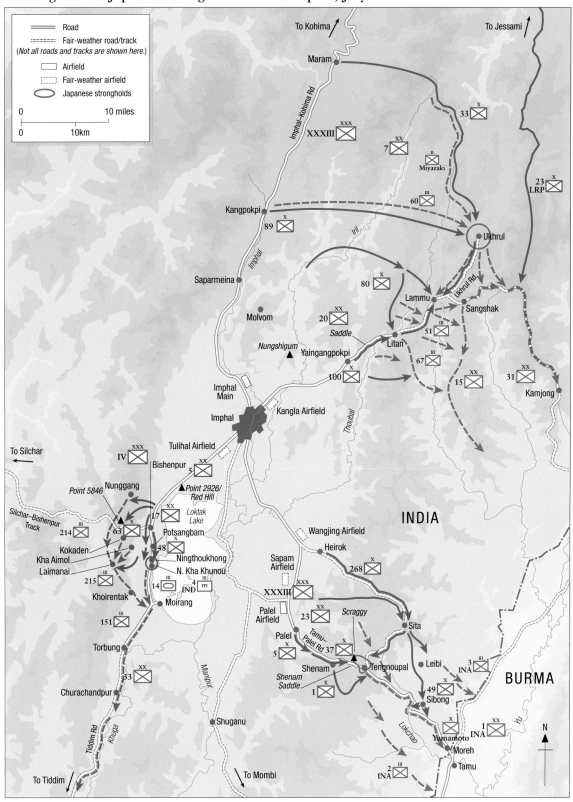

Legend:
- Road
- Fair-weather road/track
- (*Not all roads and tracks are shown here.*)
- Airfield
- Fair-weather airfield
- Japanese strongholds

0 — 10 miles
0 — 10km

To Kohima

To Jessami

Maram

Imphal-Kohima Rd

XXXIII

7 XX

33 X

Miyazaki

23 X LRP

60 III

Kangpokpi

89 X

Iril

Ukhrul

Saparmeina

Imphal

80 X

Lammu

Ukhrul Rd

Sangshak

Molvom

20 XX

Saddle

Litan

51 III

Nungshigum

Yaingangpokpi

67 III

100 X

15 XX

31 XX

Kamjong

Imphal Main

Kangla Airfield

Imphal

Thoubal

To Silchar

IV XXXIII

Tulihal Airfield

Bishenpur

5 XX

Nunggang

Point 2926/ Red Hill

Point 5846

17 XX

Loktak Lake

Wangjing Airfield

Heirok

INDIA

268 X

Silchar–Bishenpur Track

214 III

63 X

Kokaden

48 X

Potsangbam

Kha Aimol

Ningthoukhong

Sapam Airfield

Laimanai

N. Kha Khunou

215 III

14 X IND

4 III

XXXIII

Khoirentak

Moirang

Palel Airfield

23 XX

Scraggy

Sita

151 III

Palel

37 X

Tengnoupal

Leibi

3 III INA

Torbung

5 X

Shenam

BURMA

49 X

Sibong

33 XX

Churachandpur

Shenam Saddle

1 X

Manipur

Lokchao

1 XX INA

Khuga

Shuganu

Yamamoto

Moreh

To Tiddim

Tiddim Rd

To Mombi

2 III INA

Tamu

Yu

N

85

Ukhrul, taken from the air on 22 March 1944, with the road from Imphal in the foreground. Japanese forces used the road as an important communications link, and it was the target of frequent attacks by bomber aircraft of the Strategic Air Force, Eastern Air Command. (AWM, P02491.196)

THE SOUTH-EAST

On the south-eastern approach to Imphal, the two armies continued to face each other on the Shenam Saddle. Yamamoto Force remained in place on these heights and the front line was still on Scraggy. It was in the second half of July that a final, concerted effort was made to evict Yamamoto Force and push it down the Tamu–Palel Road towards the India–Burma frontier. Led by the 23rd Indian Division (now part of XXXIII Corps), the operation involved five brigades in a three-pronged attack.

The central thrust was by the 37th Indian Brigade on the Shenam Saddle, with the support of all available artillery and tanks; the 5th British Brigade was deployed behind it and readied to provide assistance. D-day was to be 24 July. The 1st Indian Brigade was sent through the hills on the right, to arrive behind the saddle. The two were to push the Japanese back on the road. It was hoped their withdrawal route would be cut by the 49th Indian Brigade, which would arrive on the road after looping in from the far left; the 268th Indian Brigade would be to its left, protecting its flank.

The attack commenced as planned. Nippon Hill and Scraggy fell on the morning of 24 July. Within two days, the two brigades of the 23rd Indian Division were advancing down the road. However, despite arriving behind the Japanese in time in the Sibong area and attempting to block the road, the 49th Indian Brigade was unable to stop the retreat of Yamamoto Force towards Moreh. The INA's 1st Division also retreated from the hills around the area in the second half of July.

THE NORTH

To the north in July, the focus of fighting was the Ukhrul area. Since the end of the Kohima battle, the 31st Division had been retreating to Burma through Ukhrul. By early July, Miyazaki Force, the division's rearguard that had attempted in vain to stall the British 2nd Division's advance from Kohima to Imphal, had arrived in the area. It was joined by the remnants of the 15th Division's 60th Regiment and Honda Raiding Unit that had also retreated here from the Imphal–Kohima Road after its opening on 22 June.

To their south were other units of the 15th Division, including its 51st and 67th Regiments, battling to ensure the road to Ukhrul from Imphal remained blocked. In the meantime, Mutaguchi had relieved the divisional commander, Yamauchi, both because of his worsening illness and also because he no longer had confidence in him. The new commander, Lieutenant-General Shibata, took over command in early July.

As June gave way to July, the Japanese around Ukhrul were faced with an onslaught from multiple directions directed by XXXIII Corps. The 33rd Indian Brigade and 89th Indian Brigade (both of the 7th Indian Division) advanced on Ukhrul from the north (Maram) and east (Kangpokpi) respectively. Columns of the 23rd Long Range Penetration Brigade (the Chindits) approached from Jessami in the north and cut off the routes of retreat to the east. From the south came the two brigades of the 20th Indian Division (the division was now brought under XXXIII Corps) – the 80th and 100th Indian Brigades. The latter brigade had been fighting to open the Ukhrul Road since the second half of May.

On 8 July, all resistance at Ukhrul was overcome and the town fell. The Ukhrul Road was reopened two days later. The Japanese survivors headed south-east from Sangshak to the frontier over the jungle-covered mountains, their passage made all the more difficult by the unending rains and harassment by Fourteenth Army's patrols. Many thousands died in the final retreat of Fifteenth Army in July towards the relative safety of the Chindwin River, an area from which they had marched forth towards Imphal with such swiftness and purpose just over four months earlier.

Present-day view of the eastern side of Ukhrul. The survivors of the Japanese 31st Division from Kohima and many of those from the 15th Division around Imphal passed through this village at the end of the two respective battles. (Author's collection)

AFTERMATH

The combined battle of Imphal–Kohima is considered the largest defeat on land ever for the Japanese Army. Although numbers vary, it is estimated that some 30,000 Japanese soldiers died and 23,000 were injured in this clash between their Fifteenth Army and the British Fourteenth Army in 1944. This includes men who died in the fighting, due to disease and in the disastrous retreat back to the Chindwin River in Burma. Of these, fatalities and those missing from the two divisions at Imphal were estimated to be over 16,000 men, while the figure for Kohima was over 6,000; another 8,000 army troops were also among the dead. Of the 6,000 men of the INA's 1st Division, about a third died and another third were hospitalized. There were over 16,000 casualties for Fourteenth Army, of which some 12,000 were sustained at Imphal.

The failure to capture Imphal shattered Fifteenth Army. The impact on the Japanese in Burma was not insignificant: a key pillar of its control and defence of that country had been roundly defeated at the hands of the British forces. The clock began to tick on the Japanese hold on Burma. For the British, it brought into play the very real possibility of retaking Rangoon by a land offensive. Slim went on to capitalize on this opportunity and directed

A Japanese war memorial at the base of the old Point 2926 or Red Hill. Its construction was funded by former comrades of those Japanese soldiers who died in the battle for this hill in May 1944. (Author's collection)

a swift offensive into Burma – the very move that Tokyo had sought to pre-empt by its Imphal operation. The Japanese in Burma were not given the opportunity to catch their breath and gather themselves. And so, when Fourteenth Army, now even more confident and sure of its abilities, poured into the country and advanced south, it was countered by a Japanese force that had been weakened following the action in Imphal. The British now had the forward momentum and they used it to take Rangoon less than a year after Imphal.

Present-day view of Loktak Lake, which lies to the east of the Tiddim Road between Bishenpur and Moirang. Visible in the distance is the western hill range overlooking the Imphal Valley, with Point 5846 at the extreme left. (Author's collection)

More than anything else, perhaps the single most important reason for the Japanese defeat at Imphal was their underestimation of their opponent's capabilities. Mutaguchi's entire strategy rested on a speedy capture of Imphal. But the army he faced in North-East India in 1944 was not the same as the one the Japanese had defeated in Burma in 1942, especially in its training, logistical support and, importantly, morale. The men of Fourteenth Army did not think the Japanese soldiers invincible. In battles large and small, they stood their ground as required, did not scatter when the Japanese tried to cut them off, and fought back, inflicting delays on the advancing Fifteenth Army and repeatedly throwing them off their tight timetable.

For an army whose soldiers were travelling light, with a tenuous supply line behind them and a hope that they would sustain themselves on their enemy's supplies, these delays proved fatal. Even on the occasions when the Japanese were able to capture British supply depots, most of the valuable

Present-day view of the old Imphal Main Airfield (locally known as Koirengei Airfield). One of only two all-weather airfields in the Imphal Valley, it was at the heart of the 'air battle' of Imphal and the sustenance of the besieged IV Corps by air supply (Operation *Stamina*). (Author's collection)

supplies had already been evacuated or destroyed. Once their advance on and around all the routes to Imphal was halted, the Japanese found themselves strung out for months over some of the most treacherous terrain in the world and with the monsoon rains upon them. The result was disaster.

It is worth noting, however, that Mutaguchi very nearly succeeded in his plan to capture Imphal, especially in the battle's opening stage. He cut off (albeit without destroying) the 17th Indian Division on the Tiddim Road and drew reserves away from Imphal, leaving Scoones suddenly vulnerable. His thrust from the north via the 15th Division was a surprise for the British. But where Mutaguchi faltered was in underestimating how swiftly the British would be able to react. For even by the time those units of the 15th Division unaffected by the battle at Sangshak – such as the 51st Regiment – arrived at the gates of Imphal, it was too late: the two brigades of the 5th Indian Division had already been flown in and were plugging in the gaps in the northern defences.

A related problem was with the 15th Division itself. Considering it was the one with the best chance of taking the primary target of *U Go* in 1944 – Imphal – in its opening stage, it was unforgivable that it was so under-strength at the start of the operation. Yamauchi also did not help matters by suddenly changing the targets of his two main columns north of Imphal. Once the 15th Division's initial efforts were rebuffed, it was never able to recover the offensive. Instructing Sato to then send a strong force to Yamauchi's aid from Kohima was always going to be difficult for the former to comply with. The opportunity to seriously threaten Imphal from the north at the start of the offensive was therefore lost because of the state in which the 15th Division had arrived at its northern gates.

Fourteenth Army's overall strategy for Imphal was a success. Slim and Scoones had wanted the Japanese to overreach and extend themselves from the Chindwin River to the Imphal Valley. Slim in particular, learning from his experience in 1942, had wanted to fight the Japanese on ground of his choosing, this time with the shorter and more secure supply lines behind his men. Although there were some scares, this plan worked. A crucial factor in Fourteenth Army's success was the support it got from the air – the many roles the Allied air forces played made the difference between defeat and victory at Imphal. Keeping IV Corps supplied by flying thousands of sorties to Manipur's airfields (Operation *Stamina*) blunted the pain caused by the Japanese siege. Other valuable support included flying in reinforcements in the nick of time (5th Indian Division); evacuating casualties; dropping supplies and ammunition; bombing Japanese supply lines; and supporting the infantry's operations.

Ultimately, of course, the task of clinching a victory was left to the soldier on the ground. It was his actions, far removed from the grand strategies of the generals, which would win the

Indian soldiers inspecting a captured field gun, 1944. (NAM, No. 74812)

day for Fourteenth Army. In that respect, Imphal was quite an Indian affair. Or, to be even more precise, an Indian and Gurkha affair. Most of the infantry battalions who fought the Japanese around the Imphal Valley were either Indian or Gurkha. Fighting alongside British units such as the West Yorks, Devons, Northamptons and Suffolks, these men from India and Nepal proved their mettle.

They also had to face a peculiar situation: fighting against their own brethren and former comrades who sided with the Japanese as part of the INA. It was only around Imphal that two formed groups of Indian soldiers – one from the (British) Indian Army and the other from the INA – clashed with each other on Indian soil in World War II. The experience was a blow to the morale of some in the INA: they had to deal with the realization that their former comrades from the Indian Army considered them traitors. Imphal was also a broader disaster for the INA. While it had little more than a nominal presence alongside the Japanese, the army had hoped that Imphal would be the crucial first step of an eventual advance deep into India. It was not to be. Poorly equipped compared with Fourteenth Army, and dependent on the Japanese for supplies, the INA units shared the fate of the Japanese.

Men of the 3/3rd Gurkha Rifles inspect Japanese ordnance on Scraggy after it was recaptured in July 1944. (Getty Images, No. 451596252)

The British in India had a close shave at Imphal, because, to be fair to the INA, the way things turned out at Imphal in 1944 meant its allure and potency as a force that could rally support among the broader Indian public was not really tested. That test would have only happened had the Japanese won at Imphal. For then, many more thousands of INA soldiers would have arrived from Burma, including its leader, Subhash Chandra Bose. He could have set foot in India and plotted his next move, with the help of the Japanese. On their part, the Japanese would have had the chance and space to consolidate their hold on the Imphal Valley and its network of supply depots and airfields.

What impact an INA-led force could have had if it had subsequently managed to reach Assam and Bengal firmly rests in the realm of speculation. But one can at least admit the possibility that the sight of Bose on his home ground at the helm of an Indian army of liberation could have been quite destabilizing for the British in India. It had the potential to fire the imagination of the masses and test the loyalty of at least some soldiers of the Indian Army. All of this could have had especially unpredictable consequences for the British, as it was a time when there was already strong public support for independence from their rule.

In the end, it never came to this. The Japanese invasion of India was repelled and the British Fourteenth Army won a decisive victory at Imphal in 1944. A turning point in the Burma Campaign was reached. A year later, the campaign itself was over, with the Japanese defeated in Burma.

THE BATTLEFIELD TODAY

The environs of Imphal are a battlefield tourist's delight. The city itself is home to two cemeteries maintained by the Commonwealth War Graves Commission. Also of interest is a colonial cottage in the Kangla Fort complex where Slim stayed for a few months in 1944. The airstrip one lands on – Tulihal – was first developed in the war. But to view the battlefields, one has to head out to the various spokes leading out of Imphal.

On the Tiddim Road, one can visit Point 2926/Red Hill, at the base of which lie two Japanese war memorials. The approach to the next major town, Bishenpur, shows the importance of its location in 1944, between the hills and the Loktak Lake. For a feel of village and paddy field fighting, the stretch from Bishenpur to Moirang is perfect. One can walk the banks of the Potsangbam *turel* to get a sense of the fighting there. Ningthoukhong has become a large town now, but one can still explore the area of the stream east of the road.

To get closer to the Point 5846 area, one can brave the winding and ill-maintained – albeit atmospheric – old Silchar Track from Bishenpur. Or trek to it along the ridgeline from Lamdan to the south (much like many Japanese had done). This allows one to see the old positions of Wireless Hill and Wooded Ridge up close; Water Picquet and Mortar Bluff off the track remain difficult to access. Note that the present-day alignment of the track near Point 5846 differs from what it was in 1944. Farther south on the Tiddim Road and just off it lies Moirang, which has the only INA memorial complex in the world (including a war museum); the site of the Torbung roadblock down the road is also accessible.

The set of battlefields that are stunning, relatively easy to access and quite unchanged are those of the Shenam Saddle. Even today these hills lie uninhabited for the most part and hugged by the Tamu–Palel Road (now called the Moreh Road). The old Nippon Hill and parts of Crete East are occupied by the Assam Rifles, but the other peaks remain more or less as they were in 1944. Recce Hill has remains of old bunkers and trenches; such reminders of the battle continue to be discovered across Manipur to this day. Most of the old Palel

Statue of Subhash Chandra Bose at the INA Memorial Complex in Moirang. (Author's collection)

Airfield has been built upon, but one can still make out its outline from the surrounding hillocks.

Heading out on the Ukhrul Road, Nungshigum and its vicinity in the Iril River Valley is also largely unchanged from the war. Driving up the road eventually gets you to Sangshak (present-day Shangshak village). While it is more built up today, one can still identify the old British and Japanese positions. Sangshak has a war memorial and remains of trenches can be found around the village. One can also go on to visit Ukhrul to the north. The surrounding mountains from both places give one a good sense of the terrain many Japanese traversed in 1944.

One can still spot trenches and bunkers dating back to 1944 on some of the hills of the Shenam Saddle and around the other Imphal battlefields. Visible here are some trenches on Recce Hill. (Author's collection)

Along the Imphal–Kohima Road, most of the old Imphal Main Airfield survives. The Mapao–Molvom Range can be seen from both this road and from the east near Nungshigum. At Kanglatongbi is a war memorial maintained by the Indian Army. From Kanglatongbi to the old Milestone 109 area is an atmospheric drive, with the Imphal *turel* flowing alongside and the hills to the east. One can get an immediate feel for the terrain and the challenge the 5th Indian Division faced to open the road northwards in 1944. Finally, it is well worth driving on up the road to Kohima to see what remains of its old battlefields and to visit the spectacular Kohima War Cemetery.

Note that Manipur is subject to sudden road closures: any travel plans to the area should involve a certain degree of flexibility. The Imphal-based Battle of Imphal Tours pioneered battlefield tours to Imphal and Kohima and can organize them through the year. They can be contacted at battleofimphal@gmail.com or via their website (www.battleofimphal.com).

Present-day view of the Imphal–Kohima Road and the low-lying hills and Imphal *turel* (river) to its east between Kanglatongbi and Saparmeina. The area was the scene of fierce fighting in June 1944 as the 5th Indian Division advanced up the road. (Author's collection)

FURTHER READING

Allen, Louis, *Burma, The Longest War*, London (1984)

Brett-James, Antony, *Ball of Fire: The Fifth Indian Division in the Second World War*, Aldershot (1951)

Brett-James, Antony & Evans, Geoffrey, *Imphal, A Flower on Lofty Heights*, London (1962)

Fay, Peter Ward, *The Forgotten Army*, Ann Arbor (1993)

Franks, Norman, *The Air Battle of Imphal*, London (1985)

Freer, Arthur F., *Nunshigum*, Durham (1995)

Grant, Ian Lyall, *Burma: The Turning Point*, Barnsley (2003)

Hudson, John, *Sunset in the East*, Barnsley (2002)

Johnson, Christopher D., *The Forgotten Army's Box of Lions*, Norwich (2001)

Katoch, Hemant Singh, *The Battlefields of Imphal, The Second World War and North East India*, New Delhi (2016)

Kirby, S. Woodburn, *The War Against Japan, Volume III, The Decisive Battles*, Uckfield (1961)

Lyman, Robert, *Japan's Last Bid for Victory*, Barnsley (2011)

____, *Kohima 1944, The Battle that Saved India*, Oxford (2010)

Molloy, Terence R., *The Silchar Track*, Ely (2006)

Prasad, Bisheshwar (ed.), *The Reconquest of Burma, Volumes I and II*, New Delhi (2014)

Rooney, David, *Burma Victory*, London (1995)

Seaman, Harry, *The Battle at Sangshak*, London (1989)

Slim, William J., *Defeat into Victory*, London (1956)

Toye, Hugh, *Subhash Chandra Bose, The Springing Tiger*, Mumbai (1991)

United States Army, *Burma Operations Record: 15th Army Operations in Imphal Area and Withdrawal to Northern Burma* (1957)

INDEX

References to images are in **bold**.